Building a Wilderness Retreat

The Wild 80

Glenn Devery

Voyageur Press

Printed in the United States of America.

89 90 91 92 93 5 4 3 2 1

Library of Congress Cataloging-in-Publication Data
Devery, Glenn, 1923–
    Building a wilderness retreat : the wild 80 : text and
illustrations / by Glenn Devery.
        p.   cm.
    ISBN 0-89658-086-5 : $17.95
    1. Country homes—Design and construction.   2. Country life.
I. Title.
TH4835.D48   1989
690′.872—dc20   89-35632
                                                             CIP

Published by Voyageur Press, Inc.
P.O. Box 338
123 North Second Street
Stillwater, MN 55082 U.S.A.
In Minn 612-430-2210
Toll Free 800-888-9653

Voyageur Press books are also available at discounts in bulk quantities for premium or sales-promotion use. For details contact the Marketing Manager.

Please write or call for our free catalog of natural history and wildlife publications.

Acknowledgments

My thanks to *Minnesota Volunteer, Outdoor Life, Minnesota Sportsman,* and *Deer & Deer Hunting* for material that first appeared in those magazines; to my diligent editor; and to Miriam, my understanding wife.

Also, thanks to publishers *Henry Holt & Co., Inc.,* for permission to use copyrighted material edited by Edward Connery Lathem, from *The Poems of Robert Frost:* "Mending Wall" and "Stopping by Woods on a Snowy Evening."

*   *   *

Author's note:
Except for obvious names of relatives and a close friend or two, I have avoided real names in these pages.

CONTENTS

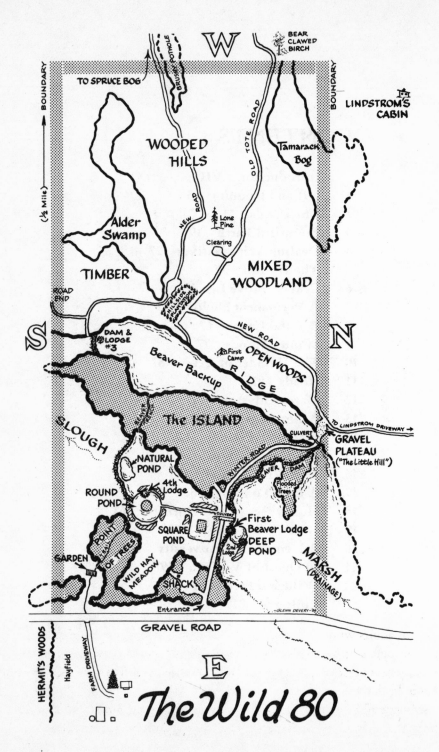

The Wild 80

Introduction

I never want to see another windowless office.

Those years downtown left me with a vague emptiness—something else begged for my attention, something beyond concrete, steel, and monetary mania.

Like Aldo Leopold, I craved the company of wild things. I longed for a hidden retreat in the forest, where I could periodically "clear the slate"—a place to inhale clean air and woodsweet smells, and let the winds sweep away the mental cobwebs of urban congestion.

In such a setting, I might pause at the edge of a cattail slough to watch a red-tailed hawk ride the thermal currents, or admire the grace of a whitetail doe when she stepped lightly down to the beaver pond for a drink. And I would be on hand for the endless intrigue of seasonal changes in the woods, from April's first emerging wild-flowers to the onslaught of winter's wind and snow.

We all have an occasional need for a quiet time, a time to be alone with our thoughts. Whether it be a closed room or a secluded place in the realm of nature, just an hour or a day by ourselves can help us reassess our lives.

Granted, some of us have greater need for solitude than others; I am one of the former. It has never bothered me to be alone, but I have known adults who are completely ill at ease when they are deprived of constant companionship. Left alone, they cannot cope with the strangeness of isolation. As far back as I can remember, I have felt at home in the woods.

My friend Ken once came upon a hunter lost in the woods. Out of breath and wild-eyed, the poor soul was seized by panic; he was overcome with joy to find another human being.

"Where did you come in?" Ken asked the man.

"I don't know . . . it . . . it all looks . . . the *same,*" he stammered.

The fellow did not know where he had left his cap, or his rifle. He cared only about one thing—getting safely out of the woods to join his companions. He had been charging around in circles, a mere two hundred yards from the nearest road! Ken quickly led him to "safety."

In my quest for private land, never did I intend to hide from the world. But even if it meant splitting my life into two worlds—city versus country—wouldn't one complement the other? As I look back, it surely has done that. To support a family, I pursued my profession of commercial art in the city. From every trip to the woods, I returned refreshed in mind and spirit. Thus fortified, I was better able to cope with the other life.

Animal behavior has always fascinated me, and I knew that with time and patience, I could catch a glimpse of the lives of wild creatures. And yet the study of wildlife was not my sole reason for wanting to own a plot of woodland. A combination of interests pointed me in that direction.

Because I am an ardent fancier of trees, that alone would have been excuse enough. And off the beaten paths, I'd find enchanting wildflowers to study. Unhindered in my woods, I could follow their progressive bloom from spring to fall.

Having spent my boyhood on a farm, I felt a need—almost an obligation—to expose our small children to nature. Of course I had no guarantee that they would like it; but I wanted them to know of a different world, far removed from suburban shopping centers. Subconsciously, perhaps I hoped to leave them a legacy of more than monetary worth.

My ancestors were hunters because wild game was crucial to their survival, and the challenge of getting close to game birds and animals taught me respect for ways of the wild. In private woods, I planned to guard the balance of game species. In fact, I intended to go a step further by improving habitat for any wildlife to be found there.

And though it was not of major importance to me at the time, I faintly sensed the wisdom of investing in land. "Don't wait to buy land—buy land and wait," Benjamin Franklin advised. I must admit, however, the rapid rise in real estate values (and taxes) has since amazed me.

Isolated residences had begun to crop up in the hardwood forest of my native corner of southeastern Minnesota. Many years of free roaming hose hills were cut off abruptly by new development and "No Trespassing" signs—and a long-dormant urge within me gained strength.

I think the last straw was my shock one day on visiting a favorite haunt . . .

A few miles from Rochester, Minnesota, the scenic Root River winds around the base of cream-colored limestone cliffs. Above bends in the river, these cliff facings present sheer drops of one hundred feet or more. Any open ground, atop the bluffs or in the bottomland, is subject to the plow. But tall Norway pines stand above oaks and birch and maples, in terrain too rugged for farming.

In one place, a long sloping hill stretched nearly a mile to the bottom of a U-shaped loop in the river. When autumn came, I could gather a bushel or two of black walnuts on that hillside, hardly making a dent in the squirrels' supply. Open fields and pasture dipped and rolled the full length of the hill. Deer browsed in brushy draws on the fringes leading to the river. My dad once found a "bee tree" on that cherished hillside, and with permission of the farmer, we harvested the honey.

The high view revealed part of the hidden bend upstream, where I often fished for bass. To reach it, I had to come down a back road from the other side, past an abandoned farm. The buildings' crumbling limestone foundations were secreted in brush and timber.

Early one morning down there, as daylight seeped into the canyon between tall bluffs, I watched a raccoon in the mist. He was absorbed in tipping over slabs of rock in the shallows, looking for crayfish. I usually did likewise, because crayfish were a weakness of the lunker bass lurking behind big rocks in the river.

These memories and more pulsated through my mind when I stared down at the manicured greens of a spanking-new golf course. Now these hills would echo "Fore!"

The deer and the foxes would have to adjust.

Building a Wilderness Retreat
The Wild 80

1 Off and Running

Each one's world is but a clearing in the forest—so much open and inclosed ground.
Henry David Thoreau

The time was ripe for me to find some private woodland. I began to explore remote acreage offered for sale, and during the next two years, winter and summer, I tromped over a lot of new ground.

These rules would govern my selection: the land shouldn't be more than 125 miles from home, and it had to fit my pocketbook—a cash deal with no finance charges. I preferred woodland off the beaten path, on a secluded gravel road. Anything close to a town would mean blacktop highway and heavy traffic.

A 40- or an 80-acre parcel would satisfy me. Although I wanted it to have a creek, I knew water cost money in any land transaction. That ruled out lakeshore property. Land with a good variety of trees would suit me fine. After all, Minnesota has plenty of lakes and streams with public access.

On a road map, I drew circles 100 to 150 miles from the Twin Cities, to help me focus on the territory I intended to look over. *North* was my only choice, because most of this state's undeveloped land lies in that direction. I gathered maps of all types from several counties. After mastering such legal descriptions as "The SE¼ of NW¼ of Sec. 19, Twp. 36, Rge. 18, Spruce County, Brook Township," I hit the road. (Gasoline was cheap in those days.)

Actually, *all* of the parcels I examined were bargains, but I didn't know it then. Anyway, profit was not the motivating force behind my search.

Every ad of potential sent me forth to the hinterlands, maps and compass in hand. I've always had a passion for exploring strange

3

terrain. However, very little of the rough land I traipsed over had discernible boundary lines. Much of it had a high percentage of wet ground, or not enough tree variety to tempt me. Other attractive plots were inaccessible.

Finally, after I ran down almost thirty months of land-for-sale offers, a Sunday newspaper ad caught my eye: "80 acres woodland, fronts road, no bldgs . . ." *Something clicked.* I reached for the phone. The man described the parcel in enticing terms: "It's about two hours' drive north . . . on a gravel road a few miles off the blacktop. Mostly woods . . ." And the price was perfect.

Because I had missed out on a few land bargains, this time I went directly to the owner's house in Minneapolis. If I risked driving north first to look it over, the piece might already be sold.

"Had quite a few calls," the seller and his wife cheerfully told me. "Several people are going up today to look at it, but you're the first to come over." And the phone kept interrupting answers to my questions. "It's on a good county road . . . part slough . . . we've never gone back into the woods . . ." The more he described it, the better it sounded.

Because I had moonlighted right through summer vacation that year, I was financially armed to take the plunge. The seller was a banker, and I'm sure he was a trifle stunned (as even I was) when I blurted: "I'll take it." Who ever heard of buying land sight unseen—without even haggling? But after all, I tried to convince myself on the way home, it's no more risky than buying a used car. And there wouldn't be any garage repair bills on land. I had handed over the check in full, gambling that I would be satisfied.

The seller probably had bought the 80 acres at rock bottom a few years earlier, although that was no concern of mine. Maybe he got it at tax forfeit rates; as late as the 1960s, to avoid paying back taxes people were commonly letting undeveloped land revert to state or county ownership. Most of them are probably still kicking themselves for being so foolish, now that inflation has bloated prices.

For the next two weeks I was on pins and needles, anxious to see the newly purchased woods. The kids (Brian, age 10; Gail, 7; and Alan, 5) were getting antsy, too. The day came at last, and the whole family went along to look at the land—"our land," as the youngsters

4

liked to call it.

In Larsville, the last town and the county seat, we stopped at the courthouse to sign papers on a quit-claim-deed title transfer. A copy of the official-looking document would be mailed to us by the Register of Deeds. "Tax is $14.48 per year," they said.

Then we were off to find the magic woods, seventeen miles farther north. Following the banker's directions, we turned off the blacktop by a country schoolhouse, and continued about three miles west on a good gravel road. The last mile north was a narrow, less-traveled road, but in reasonable condition.

When we came over a hill studded with majestic pines, I knew they belonged to someone else, but maybe we'd find some conifers in our woods. Half a mile more and I wouldn't have to hear another "How far is our land now, Dad?"

Below the hill we saw the farm indicated in the seller's diagram, and knew we had arrived. I pulled over at the side of the road, and the kiddies burst out of the car to explore.

In contrast to the wild land on our side, the farm across the road looked so civilized, with its comfortable buildings and neatly cropped hayfield. A tall spruce accented the farmyard. I'm partial to pines and spruce, but there was no sign of an evergreen on our side of the road.

Had I been fleeced? At first glance we were, as they say, "underwhelmed." Just in from the trees along the road, a strip of slough swept diagonally across our eighty acres. Between curved borders of low, wooded hills, waving weeds and grasses stretched half a mile in either direction.

"It's a *swamp*," my wife, Miriam, promptly snorted. "You've bought a swamp!"

She does have a knack for paring facts to the bare bone. I tried to assure her that we could easily get our money back in a resale— maybe even show a profit.

From the road, the land looked so *flat,* and I had envisioned all hilly woodland such as I'd roamed as a youth. Oh, well . . . I began to look for redeeming features. Two peninsulas of trees jutted into the slough from the road, with an acre of wild hay meadow in between, and the birches were lovely.

BUILDING A WILDERNESS RETREAT

It was early September, and a nice day for a charcoal cookout. We traced a brushy logging trail about thirty yards in from the road and built a fire on the edge of the meadow. The kids ran free.

Miriam was eight months pregnant, and that first day we didn't venture far inland. I went in only far enough to discover that those big trees out there were on an "island," because a strip of low ground cut through behind them. Beyond the dry slough, deep woods stood dark and silent, offering no hint of adventures to come.

Late in September, I put the land up for sale at double the purchase price. If that worked out, I could afford a "better" place. Demand for undeveloped land had begun to escalate, judging by the ads that I continued to follow out of habit.

One fellow decided to buy the 80 acres, but his wife squelched the deal. Then I had second thoughts about selling. Why not keep the land for a year or so?

In October, my brother-in-law joined me for the first campout in our woods. Rather than leave the car on the road overnight, Jim and I parked in farmer Bob's yard across the way. Bob was amiable, but I noticed a twinkle in his eye. Native residents always fight back a smile at rip-snortin' city dudes who roar up to the woods once a year to "rough it." I suppose we did look silly to them, in this era of high technology—two grown men hauling a hundred pounds of gear into the woods just to sleep in a tent overnight.

With no trail to follow, how we struggled across that tangle of slough grass and weeds. The first ridge we came to looked just fine—open woods overlooking the long tree-covered island in the slough below. When the tent was pitched and staked, we built a blazing campfire at dusk. Solitude at last.

Dawn came early after a quiet night's sleep. "Nothing beats waking up in the woods," we told each other with satisfied grins. The campfire eased away the chill of an October morning. While we warmed our hands over the crackling flames, a flock of high-flying geese honked their way southward.

After breakfast, we followed an old road into strange woods. In years past, loggers had carved a winding east-to-west tote road through this section of land. Brush and saplings had crowded into the open space of the abandoned road, making it difficult to follow. It was easy to get lost when we wandered off the trail.

On the far end of the wild 80, near a strip of tamarack bog, we found a bear-clawed birch tree. The trunk was marked about seven feet above its base. This discovery gave me a different slant on who the *real* owners of these woods might be.

At midday we broke camp and tromped back to the road with our heavy gear, wondering why we had brought along so much stuff.

Farmer Bob mentioned a bulldozer operator on the highway four miles away, and we stopped there next to see if Lester might push a rough road inland.

"Sure, $15.00 a hour," he quoted. He knew the location, and I told him to go ahead.

Two weeks later, Lester had cut a road—but only fifty yards or so.

"'Fraid I can't risk crossing the slough with a 'dozer," he explained. "Almost lost a machine clear to China one time south of there." So that was that. At least the short driveway and clearing at roadside would come in handy.

Lester had hauled in a used culvert at my request, a county road reject that I could have for $35.00. He dropped it to one side for future placement. It was months before he billed me for the culvert and bulldozing.

My daughter and I hiked back to the bear-clawed birch. I lifted her up to see the deep scratches in the bark, and we were both thinking about the size of such a bear as I lowered her to the ground. Suddenly brush snapped behind me and I reached for my shotgun. Gail shrieked, "Shoot him! Shoot him!" and I spun around ready to face a charging bear—but it was only a porcupine.

The docile porky inched his way up the trunk of a nearby tree. I cautioned Gail against touching those wicked barbed quills. They may look like a bad hairdo, but the sharp detachable spines are severely effective against the porcupine's enemies. Few would risk attacking a bundle of thirty thousand devilish quills.

One of my friends once found a puny starving bobcat with its throat full of quills. Hunger had driven the wildcat to a fatal error.

Even large cats (such as tigers in India) sometimes make the mistake of tangling with a porcupine. After such a foolish encounter, festering sores may render the attacker helpless. If he can no longer

7

capture his normal food, the tiger is then forced to seek easier prey—humans. Thus a man-eating tiger is created.

Knowing we were safe from tigers here, Gail and I looked around at trees the porcupine had been gnawing on. One oak was totally stripped of bark—limbs, trunk, and all.

The next time I came by there, something had eaten the porcupine; quills lay scattered in the leaves. Nature's way.

Things were hectic in the city that fall, and I couldn't return to examine the full eighty acres until after the baby was born on Halloween. (Another boy, Nathan, to share the woods with me.)

In my first venture past the dry slough, I had discovered with delight that the land rose and fell in wooded hills to the west. A variety of trees covered all but the occasional potholes: oaks, maple, birch, basswood, aspen, ironwood, ash, and elm. Tall timber. And along the slough borders, black willow, dogwood, alder, and hazel brush furnished the favorite foods of deer and grouse.

It pleased me to find a strip of tamarack bog shared with black spruce, balsam fir, and a few white pines. The evergreens spanned some two hundred yards. Thick alder and hazel brush growth fringed the patch. The stand of conifers made a striking contrast to the deciduous trees all around.

With a feeling of intrusion, I crept into the hushed interior of evergreen majesty, stepping lightly on spongy sphagnum, a cushion of moss under tamaracks standing tall and lacy on wet ground. Many years are needed to form this lush green carpet, and it seemed almost sinful to tread on such softness. Moss- and lichen-covered logs lay at rest under tamaracks—ancestors nourishing their offspring—and it left me with a sense of wonder.

By this time I had decided to keep the land. It was growing on me, and vice versa. I have looked back many times since, and shuddered to think that I almost sold out prematurely.

The wild 80 and I came together as strangers. At first I studied the somber woods with misgivings; but with time and patience, "our land" would reveal its hidden charms.

2 The Ponds

*Water . . . is the image of the ungraspable phantom of life;
and this is the key to it all.*
Herman Melville

There was no creek or stream on our land; we had only the miles-long slough crossing the front 40 inside our road frontage. The dry slough was part of an extensive watershed that carried spring runoff. If we could carve out ponds to contain a fraction of the normal flowage, we'd have a boon to wildlife. Rain or melted snow should keep the ponds filled.

A sizable variety of birds and animals would be attracted to the ponds—wild creatures that we might otherwise never see—adding enchantment to our campsite.

There is no denying the pacifying appeal of a placid pool. Isn't that why people are enticed to lakeshore cabins? Convenience of access is not their only excuse. They also crave the tranquilizing effect of water and its many moods. Although most of us have lost the adventurous spirit of our forebears on the high seas, we still find something soothing in a surface of water.

Whether it is a lake, stream, or pond, any water is a magnet to wildlife. Swallows skim the surface, ducks raise their broods, herons wait for frogs and minnows, mink and muskrats find a home—a long list of birds and mammals can depend on getting a drink in the heat of summer.

On a Friday afternoon in August, I left work early and hurried north to keep an appointment with the area game manager. Together we studied the slough to determine where to place ponds for habitat improvement.

It was a very dry year, and we scared up seven grouse behind the island. The birds were desperate for water, and had found a moist depression in the tall slough grasses. We also came upon a tromped swath where a bear had plowed through.

About fifty yards in from the clearing along the county road, alder and willows probed to a point in the slough. The narrowest, most solid part of the slough led toward the timbered island. Only there did the ground appear to be firm enough to form a natural barrier for a pond, and the game manager suggested that it might be the site of an ancient beaver dam. But would this part of the slough hold water? We cut a sapling, and in a low spot, shoved it down about four feet to test for moisture. It came up wet on the end, and showed traces of clay. He thought this should be an ideal place for digging a pond or two.

I drove home with visions of ponds to be dug, by one of three methods: bulldozer, blasting, or dragline. The game manager had offered encouragement: "Your prospects are good for getting cost sharing from both state and federal governments on a wildlife project."

Worth a try, I thought, and back in the city I began filling out application forms. Weeks passed. I waited. After state said OK, federal still dragged its feet. I wrote letters and made telephone calls, but bureaucrats move at their own pace.

Meanwhile, I staked out two pond shapes, and with bulldozing dismissed as too hazardous, I investigated blasting. The use of ammonium nitrate has proven successful when done by professional pond builders. I suggested this approach to Bernie at the Agriculture & Soil Conservation Service (ASCS). The county man scorned the blasting method for artificial ponds: "I'm never satisfied with the way they turn out." That left no choice but to hire a dragline operator at greater expense, even assuming the federal cost-sharing to be forthcoming. I waited impatiently.

Finally, on December 16th, the county game manager called me in Minneapolis. "Bernie at ASCS says they have funds now and will pay 70 percent of digging costs. The state will contribute another 10 percent."

I was jubilant, and called the man at ASCS to give the dragline operator the go-ahead.

"Remember, any road expense is not covered," Bernie emphasized.

ASCS and the dragline operator had confirmed the location. I knew how important this was from talking to a man two miles up the road. Jeff had a seasonal cabin on 40 acres, and his pond-digging episode went something like this: After making arrangements with a bulldozer operator, he drove up from the city to see how it turned out. *No pond.* Jeff confronted the contractor, for this retort: "Well, dammit—I dug one in there!" True—but it turned out to be on the 40 acres *adjoining* Jeff's land. My guess is that somebody acquired a free pond.

Two days later, Bernie called; the pond digging had begun. His quick call to action was explained: "If we don't use up all our available federal funds in a given year, we get a smaller allotment the following year."

That Saturday I went up to watch the dragline perform. Nearly two feet of snow covered the ground in late December, and I calculated my portion of snow removal cost in the slough. But why complain; it would only cost me 20 percent of the total.

The dragline's big steel jaws bit down into surface snow and weeds, and swung the load over to a growing pile. On the next bite, the scoop grabbed a mouthful of black soil. Heavy snow cover helped, because it kept the surface dirt from freezing deeper.

Government plans called for a pond depth of four feet at the outside edge. The peat layer was shallow, with clay under a foot of topsoil. Good news; the ponds should hold water.

According to ASCS standards, this was to be a square pond, with a small island. About forty yards south, downstream in the slough, a common donut shape with an island would form the second pond. Below that, a natural pond completed the series.

Though it pleased me to see the ponds take shape, the dragline operator completely ignored my staked design. He was probably "just following orders" from the ASCS. During a lull in the digging, I tried to convince the fellow to dig a *third* pond above the solid ground barrier over the slough. Water flowage would come from that direction, and I hoped to slow silting of the two main ponds below. I told him to dig that hole much deeper, and to forget the usual island. He fretted and balked at anything that didn't follow

13

regulations. I got the impression that he was afraid the sky might fall on him if he deviated from government policy.

Eventually, my persistence paid off, although at the time I had no idea of the surprise benefit this third pond would some day provide.

In February, the boys and I went up to examine the diggings. The mechanical monster had long since departed, and quiet prevailed over the woods and slough. More snow covered the ground, but the shapes of the ponds were unmistakable. Piles of frozen dirt around the edges consisted of clay mixed with topsoil, peat, and weeds—all neatly covered with a white blanket. We climbed down into the depression for shelter from the cold wind, and built a fire to roast wieners.

In April, we stopped at the bait shop in Larsville to buy minnows for stocking the ponds. I explained my plan to the owner, and made it clear that I didn't intend to go into bait competition.

"Fatheads are your best bet," the proprietor assured me. "They can survive winters in shallow water better'n other kinds." And he sold us a solid gallon of minnows for just two dollars.

Even the chilly drizzle didn't dampen our spirits when we pulled up to our clearing along the road. Golden-yellow moss roses bloomed in wet ground, and the birds were back, chirping about their territories. The trees showed signs of budding; in another week or two they would leaf out in warm May sunlight.

We promptly introduced minnows to the three ponds. "They multiply five or six times in a season," the bait shop man had told us; so that would draw in blue herons and other minnow-lovers of the wild. For good measure, the boys threw in a painted turtle they had brought along from Minnehaha Creek. With no adjacent lakes or streams, it seemed doubtful that a terrapin would ever find these ponds, and turtles do a good job of cleaning up the waterways.

The artificial ponds were brimful, with plenty of snow left to melt upstream—not to mention spring rains. A few ducks flew over and eyed the ponds; they knew a good thing when they saw it.

We nailed up the first wood-duck nesting house fifteen feet off the ground on a tall ash tree near the round pond, and cleared oak saplings for the ducks' flight access.

During the previous winter, I had carried on research of pond life, and ordered sago pondweed tubers. These nutlike seeds are furnished with added weights (small metal staples) so they will sink to the bottom and take root. You have only to toss a handful into shallow water here and there to get them started. Sago is a popular salad with ducks. I also planted duckwheat seed in the mud along the pond shores.

A drake mallard lifted off the round pond, and we could hear grouse drumming in the woods on all sides.

On the long slough island's north end, at the narrow point of crossing, we could not get over the water; it flowed through like a creek. The boys gladly took hatchets to hack down a few aspen trees for a makeshift bridge. It was a slippery, shaky affair, but we used a pole for support, and no one got wet feet.

In May we arrived in high spirits, with a small boat atop the station wagon. After pitching the tent in our clearing at the edge of the road, we enjoyed a campfire supper. That night, not one car passed by to disturb our privacy.

At sunrise, I crawled out of the crowded tent to stir up the campfire. Fresh deer tracks in the mud gave evidence of a curious visitor during the night.

At the edge of the trees, a ruffed grouse stood poised to take wing. I froze to admire the pure, wild beauty of this native woods bird. He stared back, typical topnotch feathers perked up in alarm and curiosity. Here were two strangers, meeting for the first time, appraising each other. From the broadside view, I could see his plumage in the brown phase—a pleasing combination of mottled browns. He began to cluck nervously, then abruptly exploded into flight. Wings ablur, the grouse tilted and dipped gracefully through the aspens toward the second point of woods across the meadow. His turkeylike tail fanned to its limit to rudder-guide him swiftly out of sight.

I opened the tent flap to rouse the sleeping kids. Right after breakfast, we dragged the boat to the square pond; Brian, Gail, and Alan reveled in rowing around the tiny island. They had to initiate the round pond too, which meant dragging the boat through heavy weeds for another forty yards. I wore hip boots, but the youngsters didn't mind being muddy to the knees.

Just as we approached the round pond shore, a field mouse panicked ahead of us and leaped into the water. There he swam madly for the island. We all laughed at his determination to save himself from the invaders. "Cute," Gail declared.

With the boat handy, we were able to reach both pond islands to plant a clover-timothy mixture in the churned-up soil. After hand-scattering the fine seeds, we raked lightly over the dirt to give them a chance to take hold. In the process, we found a few agates that had been buried for centuries.

A lone teal landed as we left the ponds to load up the car. The weary young ones slept all the way home.

3 Bountiful Earth

He who knows what sweets and virtues are in the ground,
the waters, the plants, the heavens, and how to come at
these enchantments, is the rich and royal man.
Ralph Waldo Emerson

In a natural clearing across the road from his farm driveway, Bob had plowed virgin soil for my garden experiment. When his tractor bogged down in a wet spot, he had to summon a neighbor from a mile away to free his machine. And yet Bob did not want to accept any payment for his efforts.

While I spaded and raked the garden flat, Brian, Gail, and Alan and their cousins Tommy and Brad wielded hatchets to chop a trail leading to the round pond.

The temperature climbed to ninety degrees—abnormal for an early spring day—and none of us could drink enough water. The farm pump supplied cold refreshment, and "he's gone to the pump" was the story of the day. In fact, that pump held quite an attraction for these young suburbanites. None of them had ever experienced the magic of hand-pumping water from the ground.

I inhaled the cool smell of rich black dirt turned over in spring sunlight. When finished, I leaned on the spade handle to gaze at the level square of dark soil, visualizing rows of thriving vegetables by midsummer.

Before planting garden seeds, I set in three young plum trees on the south edge of the slough. Native plums favor rich loam and lots of sun. In cutting off the top layer of tough grass and tangled weed roots, I found earthworms plentiful near the surface.

Once when I turned over a spadeful of dirt, I thought I had found the world record night crawler, but the bright salmon-colored underside identified it as a red-bellied snake. Nothing to fear—this

19

climate is much too brisk for poisonous snakes.

The red-bellied is a small snake, rarely exceeding twelve inches. It has reclusive habits, and although it is common to Minnesota, the harmless little snake is seldom found. Its chestnut-gray back is well camouflaged.

As I worked in the garden, farmer Bob's words rang in my ears: "It's acid soil in this country, but it grows good radishes."

I missed him. He and his wife had sold their farm after living there for some twenty years. Shortly before they moved to town, Bob offered to sell his place to me for $8,000—house, barn, silo, and toolshed and 120 acres of land, with about two-thirds of it cleared. I know now it would have been a shrewd investment. But at the time, it sounded like a lot of money, and I worried about upkeep of the buildings. Repairs at home used enough of my spare time. Potential vandalism of unoccupied property discouraged me further. A man from Chicago bought the farm, for either retirement or investment. Now the place stood vacant.

During our toil in the afternoon, the county assessor came by, looking for the owner of the farm across the road. I told him I thought the man lived out of state.

"If he was present on January 2nd," the assessor stated, "I could put him down for homestead rate. Otherwise, his taxes will be higher."

The next day, my planting frenzy continued. At home, I had been feeding walnuts to the squirrels for several years; now I had a choice of seedlings from several trees they had planted in the wrong places. I brought some along to transplant in our woods, the northernmost climate for growing walnut trees in this state. While I was at it, why not introduce chokecherries, too? And a few lilac bushes . . .

In the city, we had a thriving hedge of lilacs, and I dug up a generous supply of young shoots. In the process, I weighed the idea of changing the wild flora of the north by bringing in a domestic shrub. A tall lilac bush bloomed in full glory beside the farmhouse up there each spring, so I knew they could stand the winters. Mentally, I inhaled the lovely fragrance of lavender lilacs floating on a spring breeze—and the lilacs won.

The ponds were overflowing with spring drainage, and minnows in the shallows proved they had survived winter.

Black willow shoots were rapidly taking command of the two pond islands and excavated dirt ridges. Our planted red clover smothered in the shade of competing willows. At first we chopped them down, but the persistent willows won in spite of our efforts. They would not tolerate the intrusion of "tame" seeds in their territory.

In an opening near the garden, I set in a few blackberry stems where they would have plenty of room to spread. By next spring I'd know whether or not this strain of berries—and other introductions—could withstand the climate.

On a protruding knob of earth, I planted the first apple tree, a Wealthy. Then we chopped small aspen trees for posts and put up a mesh fence around the garden plot to keep out rabbits and other nibblers.

We all carried pails of water from the ponds for the garden and fresh transplants. Out on the peninsula of trees, Tommy crept close enough to watch a grouse drumming on a log.

In the campsite clearing, I scattered clover seed in the damp soil, to keep the grouse contented. And I set out a bittersweet vine for my satisfaction; I like to see the bright orange berries in the fall. (If it turned out to be a male plant, there wouldn't be any berries. It took me a long time to find out that only the female vine bears fruit. You get better results when you plant several bittersweet vines in one place, to ensure cross-pollination.)

Within a twenty-yard radius of camp, I planted two more wild plum trees, three hills of rhubarb, and four gooseberry bushes for variety. I also set out a few blueberry bushes, false bittersweet (grouse like the berries), and three weeping willow seedlings. (Later on, I even tried starting wild rice in one pond, but the muskrats ate it before fall.)

The farm girl I married found humor in my horticultural binges in the wilds. She suppressed a smile with "It's like carrying coals to Newcastle."

We set a fifty-pound block of salt on a half-buried boulder in our clearing. Eventually, the salt took on a sculptured shape from rain and the grooves worn by deer tongues. When the salt was gone, the

21

deer *ate the soil* a foot deep around the boulder. If they enjoyed salt that much, we'd bring in another block.

On the edge of a small pothole beside the farm driveway, Gail rousted a "timberdoodle." I witnessed the age-old fluttering broken-wing act of distraction, and suggested that she look for the mother's nest. Sure enough, the seven-year-old searched patiently and found it. When I heard her yelp of satisfaction, I went over to look.

"Oh-h, how cute!" Gail cooed. The hidden nest held four tiny fuzzballs with bright eyes, each birdie about the size of a walnut shell. Just then, the mother woodcock dove frantically over our heads, screaming bird epithets. The baby wookcocks darted away from the nest to scatter in all directions. In the time it takes to draw a breath, they vanished in the weeds. We took one careful step at a time, and managed to find one baby bird again, but it scooted out of sight in a flash. We then very carefully retraced our steps for fear of stepping on the hiding infants.

I carried the aluminum ladder over to see if our wood duck house had a tenant. There was no sign of a nest—just a few stray feathers from a screech owl.

On the way back to camp, I made a happy discovery—*diamond willow*! Choice clusters grew on the point of trees adjoining the wild hay meadow. For years I had searched the state for this fascinating wood, and here it was in abundance.

When the coarse gray bark of this type of willow is peeled off, it bares a white wood accented by diamond-shaped depressions of a rich rust brown. It takes time, patience, and skill to carve out those diamonds, but beautiful walking canes result. The wood is also used for novel picture frames, and even for furniture. My friend Ben, a retired cabinet-maker, would have the patience to putter with this special wood. So, hatchet in hand, I cut off some four-foot segments that flaunted the most diamonds. Finding diamond willow made my day.

With the initial splurge of planting out of my system, I turned to the natural growth around me. Here and there, wildflowers were doing their thing—some already in bloom, others biding their time. Skunk cabbage led the way, followed by bloodroot and hepatica;

violets and trillium were close behind. Marsh marigolds had unfurled their gold-on-green to brighten fringes of the drab brown slough. On the island, I almost stepped on an emerging jack-in-the-pulpit.

Drainage brooks were singing their spring song, and deep in the woods I rested on a bank to absorb the sounds of new life. From below came the soft bubbling of a miniature waterfall: a narrow cascade poured over an exposed tree root to gurgle into a tiny pool. I reached into the ice-cold water to pull out a soggy handful of twigs and last year's leaves. After the water cleared again, a beam of sunlight dazzled colored pebbles on the bottom.

I followed the brook downstream until it joined another. On the sidehill, scattered young spruce and balsam mingled secretively with hardwood trees.

On a rise in the ground where the two brooks met, I made a pleasing discovery—a wildflower of a genus I had not seen in these woods: Dutchman's-breeches. The white butterfly-shaped bloom topped lacy parsley-type leaves; each plant stood only about five inches tall. I put my nose to the blossom, but couldn't detect any fragrance. There were several more specimens nearby, growing only in this small area at the confluence of brooks, on ground high enough to suggest that they needed drainage.

There is special satisfaction in finding a wildflower in its hidden retreat. The blossoms of many woodland plants are delicate and short-lived; but from the earliest bloomers to late autumn asters, each one has its time.

Though I rarely attempt to remove a wildflower from its natural setting, I counted the number here and decided to chance transplanting one. There was a shaded wet place back in camp where I would try to place it. Very carefully, I cut a block of soil around the flower's roots with my sheath knife, and wrapped it loosely in wet moss for transport.

At the far end of the wild 80, in the tamarack bog, I found my first pitcher plant. It was nestled in a depression of moss humps, half hidden beneath a clump of alder. Colored veins ranging from pink to maroon decorated the marine-green throat of its fluted top. The plant appeared to be about ten inches tall.

This remarkable carnivorous herb has always intrigued me.

23

Because bogs and marshes don't furnish enough nitrogen for pitcher plants, they evolved into meat eaters to gain nutrition. At times, even small frogs and lizards become victims to be digested by the strange plant.

The pitcher-shaped leaves are firm but flexible, almost rubbery. They catch rainwater, which in turn traps insects, and the plant absorbs them as food. The leaf edges simply join or overlap each other to form a container. Wide open at the brightly colored entrance, the leaves narrow toward the bottom to form a small cone at the base stem. A thick growth of fine, bristly hairs lines the mouth of each pitcher—thousands of waxy-smooth microscopic hairs all pointing downward. Insects are attracted by a sweet secretion within the upper leaf rim. When an insect lands to investigate the temptation, it is unable to climb back up. After a slippery slide down into the dark funnel, the insect drowns, and the plant secretes enzymes into its water trap to digest its catch.

Why doesn't the insect fly out? Perhaps some are lucky enough to escape that way, but my theory is that the fly or insect doesn't have any cause for alarm until "splashdown," and by then it is too late.

A few insects are resistant to the digestive enzymes. For instance, one type of mosquito larvae may be seen wriggling among corpses of doomed insects in the plant's cistern.

I peered inside the mysterious pitcher. At the bottom of its dark interior, one mercury-like dewdrop gleamed enticingly. Whether it was a sample of collected moisture or a secretion of the plant itself, I'm not sure.

Of the various names applied to the pitcher plant, my favorite is "Indian dipper." In Minnesota, our species of pitcher is endowed with the scientific name of *Sarracenia purpurea*—an enchanting title for this bewitching plant.

Next year I must time my visit to find the pitcher plant in bloom, in early summer. The globe-shaped flower varies from a bright crimson to deep reddish-purple. Grown singly on a long slender stem, taller than the leaves, the flower bows shyly to avoid facing the sun.

Later that day, I took a scythe to the weeds in our camp clearing, but it bothered me to mow down elegant ferns, even though they grew in profusion. There are about seventy-five varieties of fern in Minnesota, and I found half a dozen different plumes in one small area. To extend my enjoyment of them, I dug a few for the yard at home.

Also, I moved one birch clump to the city—a chancy affair. A major difference in the type of soil can spell defeat. If you find one in wet soil, and transfer it to sandy soil, the birch will rarely survive. But in this instance, the trees took hold just fine—a rare success to make up for past failures.

The assorted wild plants and flowers that cropped up around the birch's roots amazed me: ferns, wild strawberries, violets, false meadow rue, bloodroot, wild ginger, and hepatica—all from one circular foot of soil. As an added benefit from this accidental transfer of wildwood specimens, I knew when the wild strawberries up north were ripe for picking—about one week after those transplanted to our yard.

As with domestic strawberries, the wild species peaks in June. They grow anywhere the sun reaches them. If you have eaten wild strawberries, you will probably agree—they are smaller than the garden variety, but far more tasty. Birds take full advantage of the abundant strawberries in early summer.

The boys went on a tree-chopping spree while I repaired a camp chair. My orders were: "Popple only." But in their zeal to watch trees fall, one of them cut down a four-inch maple. I went over to salvage the mistake. It was the right time. Between our campsite and the downed tree, I found a lady slipper blooming in delicate shades of pink. There were five more plants in the cluster. I was delighted to find the state flower a stone's throw from camp. And if it had not been for the boy's chopping error, I might never have noticed the flowers.

The lady slippers were smaller than the white Indian moccasins I had seen farther back in the woods. These plants were in an animal path, under trees in moist ground on the edge of the meadow. To protect this rare find, I pounded in a circle of stakes around the grouping.

Whether or not the garden yielded a bounty, I would have the satisfying comfort of wildflowers.

4 Dealing With Natives

My apple trees will never get across
And eat the cones under his pines, I tell him.
He only says, 'Good fences make good neighbors.'
Robert Frost

That fall, I made a chance call to Bob's son Dick, because he owned 80 acres joining our land on the west end. If he should decide to sell in the future, I wanted him to know that I was interested.

"Why, matter of fact," Dick replied, "we put it up for sale last spring. No buyers yet. It's listed with a realtor, but maybe I can get a release from that."

A week later, Dick and I met at Tomahawk Lake, and he accepted my offer. The price per acre was double my previous purchase, but still a good deal. We made verbal agreement in the car; I gave him a down payment, with paperwork to follow.

While we chatted, an acquaintance of Dick's stopped to say hello. As it developed, Elmer owned a bulldozer, and I asked if he could plow a road through our woods.

"I live near there," Elmer said, "so let's go take a look at it right now." And he followed us up to the place. Quite a morning for wheeling and dealing, I told myself.

Elmer gazed across the wet slough toward the island. "After the ground freezes, I'll have Jake, my operator, bring in the D-7 . . . give you a call coupla' days ahead of time," he promised. His rate was $25.00 per hour.

My wife didn't share my enthusiasm for the acquisition of more land. We were not that wealthy, I was reminded. "Another bottom-less pit," she called it. Of course *I* didn't see it as a place to throw money away. This addition doubled our roaming territory into a mile-long strip of woods to explore.

27

After paying one-third down, I couldn't back out of the land deal now. With the kids on my side, their mother resigned herself to being married to a hopeless woods wanderer.

Monetarily speaking—whether by luck or by providence—within three months I sold magazine articles that covered the exact purchase price of the second 80. No interest. No carrying charge. We already owned it free and clear. Taxes then were negligible.

Although I don't take credit for any prognostication, a few years after purchase of the first parcel, unimproved land values had escalated to about fifteen times the initial investment. I have never been blessed with that rate of return from dabbling in the stock market.

The October woods were in full glory when Brian, Tommy, and I hiked back to study the "new" 80's terrain. The hills loomed higher toward the west as we followed the meandering tote road. I made a guess at the far edge of our boundary, somewhere on the highest hill back there.

Another half mile of woods brought us out on a dead-end gravel road, and from the hilltop we paused to admire the view. The scene qualified for a calendar picture: a small stream winding through the valley, with white farm ducks paddling in contentment under the bridge. On the opposite side of the stream down there, the house and barn were backed up by open pasture ringed with timber. All around it, rolling, wooded hills glowed in reds and golds of deciduous trees, accented by dark green spruce.

When the boys and I crossed the bridge to the farmyard, chickens cackled and scattered. Two dogs ran out to greet us, barking and wagging their tails.

I had been told about Charlie: "Sharp operator," they claimed, "count your change." He raised beef cattle, and ran a sideline in maple syrup. Charlie was a short, muscular man, with a round, red face. His gray-blue eyes darted all over as he talked in rapid fire.

On our first meeting, I didn't let on that I had seen his blue plastic bags hanging from maple trees in my freshly acquired back 80. Anyway, tapping a hard maple does no harm to the tree if it is done properly.

Charlie inquired: "What is that fenced-in place you got by the road over there?"

I said, "You mean the garden?"

He laughed, "Oh . . . *that's* what it is . . . I thought maybe you set out a *bear trap!*"

We headed into Charlie's pasture to swing across the stream on our way back. When we were half way across the open sidehill, Charlie yelled from the barn door, "Watch out for the bull!"

The boys and I stopped in our tracks. "*Now* he tells us," Brian muttered. We stared at the herd of cattle—mostly steers, and a few heifers, watching us with dumb curiosity. There must be a bull in the bunch someplace. Although two of us carried shotguns, it wouldn't be neighborly to shoot his bull . . .

Having been chased by mad bulls before, I knew I did not care for any such entertainment again. With a wary eye, we proceeded around the herd. Charlie's bull watched us in sullen silence, but didn't test our running speed. With a sigh of relief, we topped the hill out of view of the cattle.

On the long return trek, we took our time, savoring the aroma of autumn woods. Once in a while a grouse flushed; and near the trail, partly hidden, a doe stood still to watch us pass.

Back in camp that afternoon, we had visitors. The Lindstrom brothers stopped by to get acquainted. Both had the blue-eyed-blond look of Scandinavians; their name was familiar to me from the county plat map.

"Our 80 joins yours on the north," they said by way of introducing themselves. "We bought it when Bob let it go for back taxes. He knew about it, 'cause the sheriff called him first. But he'd already taken the saw timber and pulpwood, so he just said: 'Let 'er go.'"

In the morning, a battered pickup truck rattled to a halt beside our parked car. A tall, lean man strode into our clearing. He had kindly brown eyes and a thin, high-bridged nose and was dressed in the garb of a woodsman: battered cap, plaid shirt, faded jeans, and heavy boots.

"I'm Fabre," he introduced himself. "They call me the Frenchman."

He was looking for a place to cut pulpwood. At $3.00 a cord for popple, it wouldn't be very profitable to me, but the fringe benefits were good. What did I have to lose? Unless aspen is harvested at

29

maturity, decay sets in, and the soft wood becomes useless for lumber or processing into paper. For his cutting and hauling efforts, the logger could get $17.00 per cord at the sawmill six miles away. I liked the idea of thinning the aspen to improve habitat for deer and grouse. The whitetails would thrive on new sprouts in a clearcut. The Frenchman gave me his address in Larsville; we could work out details later.

Two fingers were missing from Fabre's scarred left hand—not uncommon to men who work with saws in the lumber business. The Frenchman must have seen our awkward stares, because he volunteered an explanation with an easy laugh: "I made a mistake when I was a kid—standing with my hand over the end of a shotgun barrel when it went off."

*   *   *

The ground froze solid in November, but Elmer's rig was "tied up on a major job." Promises, promises. I was anxious to bulldoze a road into the woods for two reasons: the Frenchman couldn't get back there to cut pulpwood on the original tote road, and my friend Red in Larsville wanted to haul out ten cords of firewood. The stacks were west of the island, and it would be impossible to get a truck over there without a cleared trail.

December came, and I began to wonder about the reliability of heavy equipment operators. The Frenchman's log skidder was on the blink, and his friend Pudge couldn't get that blankety-blank bulldozer running. If he ever succeeded in starting the 'dozer, Pudge would plow a road for us.

It was January before Elmer called, ready for bulldozing. With high hopes of getting some roadwork done at last, I drove north early the next morning.

At 8:30 I heard the rumblings of a heavy machine coming down the road. Two men pulled up with the 'dozer on a flatbed trailer. Elmer said: "This is Jake, my operator." Jake grunted at the formality, started the rig, and drove it down onto the road. With two feet of snow on the ground, he first cleared a turnaround area at roadside. Without knowing it, he bladed off a young pine I had been nursing along.

Before Elmer left in his truck, we made a deal on two concrete culverts that he would drop off.

Once the big motor started, Jake couldn't hear anything I said, so I charged ahead through the snow, pointing road direction as he plowed across the island. Although we avoided the biggest trees, the bulldozer crunched and groaned over trunks a foot thick. Frozen trees snapped off with a loud crack under the leaning weight of the heavy machine.

The slough beyond the island didn't worry Jake. He shoved safely across, and began to clear the old logging road up the hillside. It felt good to see the road take shape. Walking on freshly exposed black dirt was a relief after trudging through deep snow. Even winter boots felt light on my feet.

In one busy day, the 'dozer plowed a twisting trail to the end of the 80 acres—more than half a mile, because of the terrain. To complete the day, Jake cleared an acre of hillside overlooking the slough island. I wanted to plant pine seedlings there in the spring. The temperature climbed to forty degrees by afternoon, mild for January. At dusk, we were both glad to call it a day. I drove home, tired but satisfied.

During February, I hiked in on the new road. Fresh snow covered the dirt and uprooted trees, and there were tracks of deer, fox, snowshoe hares, and a coyote. The animals didn't mind taking the path of least resistance either.

In April, I planted a mixture of clover and timothy with a hand-casting seeder. The idea was to prevent erosion of the new woods road and to feed wildlife.

It was November again when the Frenchman sauntered into camp to discuss once more his long-delayed pulp-cutting prospects. The back 80 held the most concentrated stands of mature aspen, but our major bottleneck was the lack of a road back there. Hauling logs out the west end would be the shortest route to the sawmill—that is, *if* we could get a road bulldozed, and *if* we could have permission to cross someone else's land.

Fabre still insisted that his friend Pudge would bulldoze a road for us, free of charge. The only problem was, the guy could never get his rig running. To me it sounded as if that big machine just sat and sulked in between breakdowns.

I knew the name of the landowner joining my land to the west, although I had never met him. Fabre and I decided to drive over there to have a look—four miles by back roads.

A log-hauling truck was parked on the hill overlooking Charlie's farm, and we heard the roar of a chainsaw. The landowner lived fifteen miles away, but purely by luck, we happened to catch him there.

Fabre was reluctant to enter posted woods, especially during hunting season. I was wearing my red coat, but he had on a blue denim jacket. The two loggers probably thought we were deer hunters, ignoring the signs on the road. Waving "peace," we introduced ourselves. The boss of the operation was instantly clear to us. He eyed these brash intruders as he would burglars about to steal his heirlooms. We were interrupting his efforts to cut down oaks for sawlogs.

The Frenchman asked about chances of driving his log skidder out that end for a shorter route to the sawmill.

"No," Percy snapped. He didn't want anyone driving through his woods.

I then suggested using his border along the neighbor's pasture fence. Part of it was already cleared for a road. Nope. Not interested. If we put in a road, he feared hunters would swarm into his woods. (And maybe carry off an oak tree or two.)

I then offered to buy a strip of land along the south border, just wide enough for the road. I would maintain it for truck travel, rough but serviceable, and he could also make use of it. I even promised to put up a locked gate, with a "Private" sign. Percy still shook his head negatively. Nothing proffered made a dent in his armor. OK, thanks anyway. It looked hopeless, so we turned to leave.

To our surprise, Percy abruptly softened a trifle. Well, possibly he would let us haul pulp logs along the border fence, but only after he and I got together to survey the inland half on the south side. That was hilly and brushy for 440 yards.

"Maybe we can locate the corner where our land joins," he suggested.

32

There had to be something in it for him. Percy and I exchanged phone numbers, and after deer season we would attempt surveying. I could tell he'd be fun to work with . . .

Out on the road, the Frenchman scowled, "He's a tough one."

I nodded. "Reckon he plans to become a lumber tycoon?"

Fabre chuckled, "I'll bet that's it." And we came away with clouded hopes of gaining a shorter route to the sawmill.

Two weeks later, with mixed feelings, I drove over to keep my appointment with Percy on *his* turf. It was time to survey our mutual boundary on the west end.

Considering our first meeting, I found him in reasonably good spirits. Not that he believed in wasting time cracking a joke, mind you. This was serious business.

Percy made claim to some experience in surveying (I certainly didn't), and although he had no transit, we methodically set forth. The first forty acres (440 yards) was already open along the pasture fence, west to east. The critical half followed, from the fence corner east, up and down brush-covered hills. He "sighted" every twenty yards, and I played dummy, moving left or right a foot or so as he directed from a distance.

Thick brush made sighting difficult, but at intervals I marked boundary trees with a hatchet. Also, I had brought along a sixty foot chain with a pole at each end. This, I thought, would be a handy way to keep track of yardage.

"Nonsense!" Percy growled. He informed me that the land changes pitch so often you could lose distance *up* or *down*. My surveying ignorance was not to be overlooked.

We plodded through the snow and counted yards, repeating the total to each other as we progressed. I even marked it in the snow every forty yards. That paid off once or twice when Percy disagreed with my count. He went back to check the figure.

At last we came to the 880-yard "corner." *This was it*—something like raising the flag on Iwo Jima. He tied his blue ribbons on the tree closest to our historic boundary. I hatched-blazed the bark, and added a *red* ribbon. Now if only we had a white one to make it complete, I thought—the all-American effort.

One thing did result in my favor. The western boundary (as we arrived at it) turned out to be 150 yards farther back than I had estimated. Next, we considered trying to mark off the north to south boundary, but without a transit, Percy ruled out the idea. Maybe some other time.

I removed my kid gloves (so to speak) and returned to camp, wondering what had been accomplished. Even now, I had no more than an "iffy" commitment from him to use the roughly surveyed boundary for a road.

As it turned out, I never saw the abrasive Percy again. He eventually sold his land, and turned to digging cesspools for a living.

That winter, Fabre finally cut some popple and hauled logs out Lindstrom's driveway.

In the spring, we tromped through mud and last year's matted-down weeds to the end of the 80 to see what the Frenchman had accomplished. If nothing else, the stand of thinned-out aspen would give us a firebreak.

Judging by the open sky and stumps that greeted us back there, Fabre had harvested several cords of pulpwood. The aspen strip ran northeast from the old logging road toward Lindstrom's cabin. Green popple limbs cluttered the cleared area, and hungry deer and hares had made good use of the cutover strip that winter.

We followed the rutted trail up to Lindstroms' clearing. There an impressive pile of popple logs waited for transport to the sawmill. The Frenchman's skidder rig had left deep ruts in their dirt road, and I hoped the fellows wouldn't tar and feather me the next time we met.

Warm spring days are slower in coming to the northland, and this time we decided to foresake the tent for a warm room in town. The only building in Larsville that passed for a hotel was a large house converted for permanent roomers. They had one small room on the third floor for transients. There it was our all-night privilege to breathe stale cigarette smoke from the rooms below.

Come morning, Alan, Tommy, and I were more than ready for fresh air. After breakfast in town, we went over to the Frenchman's trailer house.

"Took out seven cords o' popple," he grinned, "and then my skidder broke down."

And that was all the pulp he ever cut in our woods. After a three-year delay, I was richer by $21.00.

No trip through Larsville, the "last chance" town en route, was complete without several stops: the bakery, our favorite cafe, and the hardware store because we always managed to leave something at home.

The small-town general store drew us in like a magnet. This time-worn building on the outskirts housed everything from tools to stoves, from candy to wolf traps. The barn-size old-fashioned store exhibited no fancy showcases, and the simple board floor tied in with its folksy character. There was no hustle and bustle, or blinding fluorescent lights, or lackluster service. The seasoned clerks were *polite*. It put us a step back in time to a more leisurely era.

When we came out of the general store this time, I saw a familiar face—Charlie was reaching into the trunk of his car, selling maple syrup, and hadn't noticed me yet. I went over to needle him a bit.

"Hello, Charlie . . . peddling syrup?"

"Hi . . . you bet; sell you a gallon?"

"No, I thought maybe you oughta' *give* me a gallon or two, after tapping my trees back there."

He looked surprised: "Uh-h . . . I don't think I went in *that* far . . ."

And I continued: "I bought Dick's 80 behind mine."

"You did?" he flushed. Then he stiffened and growled, "You try carryin' them heavy pails o' sap sometime, in snow 'n mud, up wet sidehills . . . it's a big pain in the ass—"

To avoid starting a feud, I bought a quart of pure maple syrup from him. Anyway, I was satisfied with ruffling his feathers. After that, we never again found bags or buckets hanging on our sugar maples.

5 The Hermit

Shall I, like a hermit, dwell
On a rock or in a cell?
Sir Walter Raleigh

He lived in a rundown cabin on 40 acres, less than a mile from our camp. I had heard about "Crazy" Swens—a hermit, they said: "Goes on some wild drinking sprees." Yet no one sounded afraid of him.

Toward sundown of a spring day, I decided to get acquainted with our northwoods neighbor. The boys were frolicking around the slough pond, so I walked down the gravel road to see if Swens really *was* crazy.

His tired-looking buildings sat on the high part of a flat-sloped hayfield, about two hundred yards back from the road, sheltered on three sides by trees and brush. Judging by the weathered gray boards on the cabin, garage, and shed, none of the wooden structures had ever known paint. A faint double track led through hay stubble toward the sparse set of buildings.

The place looked deserted; there wasn't a domestic animal in sight—no dog to keep him company, not even a garden. What the recluse did to occupy his time was beyond me. But maybe they said the same of Thoreau?

A thin streak of blue woodsmoke drifted out of his chimney, so I walked up and rapped on the screen door. The inner door creaked open, and I greeted "the hermit." He didn't *look* crazy: a white-haired, small, wiry man, stoop shouldered, dressed in faded overalls with suspenders, a plaid shirt, and country shoes. I guessed his age at seventy or more.

Instead of inviting me in, the old man stepped outside. I explained my presence, and he appeared to enjoy having a visitor, even a

37

part-time neighbor. In fact, Swens turned out to be quite a talker—in a heavy Swedish accent. I studied his leathery face and kindly blue eyes, and wondered how on earth he rated his nickname.

"Ya-ah . . . I wuss born over dere," he pointed through the thick shelter of trees toward the empty farm buildings hidden from our view. His parents had homesteaded that farm. I asked him if he knew the place had a new owner.

"Ya-ah . . ." His eyes lowered, and I waited for him to continue. It came as a shock when he said softly: "Bob died. Heart attack, yust last win-ter. Real nice feller, tew." I fully agreed.

We changed the subject, and it developed that the old man had worked in Minneapolis much of his life before retiring up here to home territory. The self-styled hermit didn't own a car, but he showed me a vintage tractor in the shed. "I don't ewss it much any-more." A brother lived out on the highway, five or six miles toward town, and Swens sometimes walked over there to visit. He said local people gave him a lift if they happened to pass him on the road.

Then he told me about the single, tall spruce growing beside the homestead house where he grew up: "My little sister t'ought we should have an evergreen near da house, so we went intew da woods an' came back wit' dat seedling. It grew pr-r-it-tee gyud, tew." He looked pleased at the memory.

The gentle woods dweller described a forest fire he had watched rage through timber across the road years before: "I wuss yust a boy den. Fer a fyew nights, it wuss lit up like a big cit-tee over dere—" (In parts of our woods, black and jagged pine stumps verify the tale.)

The hermit might have talked all night, because he held a wealth of information about this locale, but by dusk I had to break away and head for camp. Boys need somebody to ride herd on them, lest their exuberance lead to pursuit of mischief.

On our next trip, we stopped in to see "Crazy," and found him out in his yard cutting firewood the old-fashioned way, with a Swedish crosscut saw. I wondered aloud why he didn't use a modern chainsaw.

"Sometimes I *dew,*" he replied, "but I got tew sell it."

I thought he might be running short of funds, and I had been thinking about buying a chainsaw. He went into the shed to get it.

"How much?" I asked.

"Oh . . . t'irty dollars."

It was a very early model, heavy, with a twenty-four-inch bar. I had never used a chainsaw before; I looked it over, and he said I could have it for $25.00. Then he went through a ritual of tricks aimed at getting it running. That took a while, even for him. I began to understand why he had been sawing by hand. It finally started, and roared like an airplane motor! Too late now to welsh on the deal.

Who said he was crazy? I never did get that unruly contraption going again. Finally sold the clunker for $17.00, and how glad I was to get it out of my sight. Soon after, I bought a new chainsaw, a much lighter model—and one I could *start*.

In October, I drove up alone and stopped to visit the hermit again. It was late afternoon, and for the first time, he invited me inside. He sat peeling potatoes with a jackknife.

The one-room cabin held only bare essentials: an old iron bed, an antique woodburning cookstove, a small painted cupboard, a table and a chair or two on a scuffed-up linoleum floor. But his simple cabin was clean and tidy.

The old gent never succumbed to the charms of the telephone and electric lines strung past his road frontage. He showed no interest in radio or television, and he survived without indoor plumbing. His water came from the pump outside.

During the past summer, I hadn't seen much of him, and Swens had news: "When I wuss gone tew town, 'dey broke in 'n stole all my *gunss*," he lamented. For fifteen years he had lived on this 40 acres, and nobody had bothered him before. "Issn't like it yewss tew be." I could only sympathize with him.

"And da *shiners* [nighttime deer poachers] are t'icker . . . I seen 'em go down da road wit' spotlights." He wouldn't risk reporting it, he told me firmly. Living alone in the woods, he felt vulnerable to vengeance.

October nights were getting cool. After his tales of thieves and renegades in the area, pitching a tent had less appeal. I asked Swens if he'd mind my sleeping in the car in his yard that night. First I drove down the road to cook supper in camp. Vandals had torn down two of my "No Trespassing" signs.

Just before dark, I drove back to the hermit's yard and crawled into my sleeping bag in the station wagon. Before long, only the soft golden light from his kerosene lamp staved off the blackness of night.

About 2:00 A.M. I awoke, staring into a flashlight. *Trapped by the bandits* crossed my groggy brain, but it was only Swens: "If yew git cold, why don't yew come inside?" I assured him I was comfy, and went back to sleep.

South of Crazy Swens's an inviting dirt road led to the east from the tall pine hill. For a long time, that road had beckoned me, and one day the boys and I drove in to find out where it went. Behind the hermit's 40 we parked in a narrow hayfield bordered on one side by a row of mature spruce. Three deer bounded into the brush when we slammed the car doors.

A dilapidated log cabin slouched on the high side of an open slope. The cabin's base logs were decaying, and the low-pitched roof sagged beyond salvation. All windows were boarded up.

We felt like trespassers, but couldn't resist a look inside. The small entrance-room door was missing, and the inner door tilted open on one hinge, so we eased our way in. It was dark in there, spooky, the interior a shambles. The floor dipped and heaved in warped variations of three feet off level. Holes of ground-dwelling varmints led under the rotting floor boards.

The ancient cabin had two rooms, and one held a pair of iron-frame beds. The mattresses—what remained of them—were a mouse family's paradise. In the kitchen stood an antique cookstove in workable condition. I could imagine happy times here in the past, when hunters gathered on a cold November night for a hot supper and a rollicking poker game. Those heavy chinked logs must have vibrated with ribald laughter.

Along the gravel road between the hermit's place and our camp, there were agates for the picking. We eventually traced the source to a gravel pit a few miles away, near the Rock River. Conditions there were even better for so-called Lake Superior agates. The pit was most productive after a rain. Since no two agates are the same in size, color, shape, or design, the semiprecious stones hold great fascination for rockhounds.

Off the highway on a sideroad leading to the gravel pit, we sometimes visited a "haunted house," as the kids dubbed it. They liked to pretend it was full of ghosts—memories, perhaps, but no spirits appeared during the daytime.

The old house lurked in the trees on a shady hillside. Weathered silver gray and forlorn, it dozed in structural senility. The abandoned house nursed the history of happier days when noisy children clamored up its steep wooden stairs on their way to bed.

Living must have come hard for the early settlers, laboring from dawn till dark to gain sustenance from the soil. Here they were born, baptized, married—and possibly buried. These secrets were locked in the heart of the crumbling homestead, and its shattered windows seemed to peer back at us in silent wonder at this intrusion.

Part of the roof had collapsed to rest on the upstairs floor, and loose boards creaked and groaned in the wind. Moldy magazines from decades past littered the rooms; remnants of mildewed, rotting furniture were strewn about. Under a pile of debris, one of the boys found a battered kerosene lantern, rusted beyond recovery.

The damp earthen cellar had stored the family's winter supply of home-canned vegetables and preserves. Fragments of broken blue jars lay scattered in the dirt.

In the back yard, rocks and weeds hid a junkpile of bottles and rusty cans. Bent runners of a child's wooden sled stuck out of the pile. And in the old shed farther back in the trees, part of a dry leather harness still hung on a nail, in tribute to the horse of yesteryear.

Brush and tall weeds obscured any semblance of the former yard and garden. Only a ten-foot lilac bush remained to reveal the taste of the former inhabitants.

Between the weary shell of a house and the road out front, a gravel cut showed signs of recent excavation. It might only be a matter of time before the hill supporting the "haunted house" would be hauled away.

On a sunny day in May, I pulled in to see Crazy Swens. He had spent the winter in Minneapolis, and his blue eyes sparkled with pleasure at having someone to talk to again. After the initial palaver, Swens told me about his trip to the hospital.

"Ya-ah . . . I broke m' hip last win-ter," he stated quietly. "I wuss yust eatin' in da rest-runt, an' when I got troo, I started tew git up 'n I fell offa da *chair*—" He spoke with an air of incredulity, as if he still found it hard to believe that a simple thing like that could break a bone.

"Just from falling off a chair?" I repeated dumbly, and he nodded.

I told him my grandmother had gone through a similar ordeal, but I didn't tell him that she never recovered.

"I walked back tew da apart-ment," Swens continued, "an' den da pain got worse. So I got some med-dih-sin tew ease da pain."

Incredible! "Didn't you go see a doctor?" I queried.

"No-o-o . . ." he shook his head; "I t'ought it wuss prob'ly yust bruised, an' would git better in a fyew dayss."

In this day and age, I thought, when most people run to a doctor every time they get the sniffles, this tough old-timer had tried to treat his own *broken hip*. At last I asked, "How long did you wait, before—"

"About twelve dayss . . . but da *pain* got so bad, I fine-na-lee called da hos-pit-tal, an' dey took me in."

"You must have been laid up most of the winter then?"

"Ya-ah, I wuss. Dey had tew put a pin in m' hip tew hold it togedder." And as an afterthought, he added, "Expensive, tew!"

I left there shaking my head at the old man's capacity for punishment.

Not long after that, Swens decided to forsake his lonely cabin for the comforts of life in town. A year or so later, while I was making the usual stops in Larsville, it occurred to me that for some time I hadn't seen Swens on the street. We occasionally bumped into one another for a chat. I always offered him a ride up to his 40, but he never accepted.

At the weekly newspaper office, a block from the rooming house where the reformed hermit lived, I asked if they knew him.

"I think he might've died," the lady said, "but you could ask at the funeral parlor around the corner."

Over there, they consulted their records. "Yes . . . here it is . . . he passed away; funeral was last October."

Very businesslike. I thanked them and walked back to the car with thoughts of my own.

Half an hour later, on the county sideroad, I drove past the hermit's place. His buildings looked bleak and gloomy to me now. The twin doors on his dilapidated shed hung open, at the mercy of the wind. And the tractor he'd been so proud of was gone. The old-timer's quaint accent echoed: "Issn't like it yewss' tew be . . ."

6 Beavers Move In

By the work, one knows the workman.
Jean de La Fontaine

Changes lay ahead. Beavers had taken over the ponds! Now I could study the aquatic engineers firsthand.

That first spring, the beavers amazed us with their rapid expansion of the ponds. A new dam stretched from the deep pond to the north end of the island. There, across the narrow neck of slough, they had utilized our temporary footbridge as a piling base. Allowing for curve distance, the busy builders had constructed over two hundred yards of dam. Rocks, peat, mud, and sticks made it solid enough to back up water to the gravel road above our camp. Over five acres of slough turned into a water impoundment.

A trench—consistently eighteen inches deep anywhere I measured—followed the dam's contour. Beavers would use the canal for transporting branches in the fall. So far, I saw no sign of a lodge.

The metal culvert, once high and dry, now lay submerged and useless. We'd have to find a way to move it later.

This new development prompted us to reestablish camp on the highest ground between the ponds and the road. That meant clearing brush and small trees with hatchets, axe, machete, and grubhoe. We almost outworked the beavers that day.

A young boy in the city might balk at bringing in the newspaper, but in the woods with a hatchet, he is a wonder to watch. Once, while resting, I counted up to two hundred strokes before Nathan yelled, "Timber!" and a four-inch popple hit the ground. A man with a sharp axe could accomplish it in two or three swings, but why take away the boy's fun?

The hard-earned clearing, secluded and woodsy, pleased us all. Tall aspens shaded our campsite, and there were birch, oak, ash, maple, and linden trees all around. The green tent made it "home." Hazel brush, alder, and willows blocked our view of the ponds, so we slashed a trail in that direction, and a path to the car out on the road.

Before dark, the boys spaded a notch in the dam to test the beavers' skills.

First thing in the morning, they raced over to see if it had been plugged. Certainly. Those wetback engineers meant to conserve water.

A classic cluster of eight birch trees between camp and the ponds needed protection from beaver teeth. I wired a yard-high circle of mesh fence around them. The gnawing rodents give aspen top priority, but they will occasionally take a birch—if only to get the tree out of their runway. With those oversize choppers, beavers could probably cut through a lightweight fence, but the mesh somehow deters them. Beavers' self-sharpening, powerful incisors must be worn down by constant use, because growth never stops.

Can you imagine confronting one of their toothy, prehistoric ancestors, which were eight feet long and weighed seven hundred pounds? Fifty pounds is average for present-day beavers, but the biggest adult on record weighed 110 pounds.

Alan and I built a blind near the beaver lodge; he wanted to get as close as possible. At dawn or dusk, we became avid beaver fans, hiding in the weeds. If one of us moved, a broad tail slapped water. Sometimes the beaver dove under quietly, and sometimes it went down with a loud "slap-bloop."

Oversized lungs increase distribution of oxygen in a beaver's bloodstream. It is thereby capable of lengthy underwater excursions before it must come up for air. A clear membrane shields the animal's eyes against water, and its ears and nostrils close off like valves. Also, two inner "lips" seal the beaver's throat while it is swimming. Even so, a beaver cannot stay submerged more than fifteen minutes.

Contrary to popular belief, a beaver caught under water does not drown, as any other animal would, because its nose and throat membranes stay closed to prevent water intake. A trapped beaver's oxygen supply is gradually dissipated until the animal slips into unconsciousness and an almost euphoric demise.

Under the ice, beavers leave air pockets when they exhale. After the water converts the air bubble to oxygen, they can make use of it again.

We found clear imprints of wide-webbed hind feet in the mud along the dam. And once I discovered a scent mound where a beaver made a small pile of mud and grass to deposit a sample of *castoreum*— musk gland secretion. The creamy, orange-brown substance is just a social calling card, not any kind of warning.

After a heavy rain, beaver back-up threatened to overflow their dam. We dug a gap in it to see how the four-legged engineers might react. The sound of running water will invariably trigger beavers into action. They have been known to plaster mud over a loud-speaker when it gave forth the recorded sound of trickling water.

That evening, two beavers came out to examine the leakage. The first beaver seized a discarded stick in its teeth and forced it into the mud at the edge of the gap. The second animal followed suit. They alternated sticks with gobs of marsh roots torn loose from below. Each beaver carried a tangled mass against its chest when it swam up to work on the opening. They used their massive heads as well as their paws to shove the filler into place. It didn't take them long to stop the flowage.

Gail and I went back to start a campfire, and Alan hid in the makeshift blind at pond's edge. He postponed supper to await his chance, and finally succeeded in getting a flash photo of a beaver at work.

By the middle of June, the gravel road was flooded where it crossed the slough north of our driveway. An occasional car came through a foot of water.

"Will they dynamite the dam now?" the boys worried aloud.

That very day, trucks and a roadgrader rumbled up to solve the problem. A county road crew unloaded gravel until the road was built up a foot higher. For the time being, we thought this improvement should keep the beavers safe from being moved, or killed.

During the summer, our beavers were content with succulent shoots, and seldom took down a popple. Beavers "dine out" until freeze-up, and feed on their reserves only when it becomes necessary. As soon as the air turned crisp in September, storage activity began. Aspen bark contains more nutrients in autumn, and aspen branches cut in the fall do not have time to decay under water before the bark is eaten.

This family had started a lodge on the edge of the deep pond—the one I had insisted on being dug "to catch silt." Gobs of mud and fibrous peat were intermixed with tooth-marked peeled poles to form their home for the coming winter. Day by day (or rather night by night), the packed mound expanded. After a beaver lodge freezes solid, not even a grizzly bear can dismantle the structure. (And even if it could, the occupants would escape under the ice.)

Aspen trees and alder clumps were disappearing from around the ponds. The deep pond now had branches piled in the center, with heavy butt ends of limbs anchored in the mud bottom. Swimming beavers turned the pond water a cloudy brown.

By this time the amphibious clan had become accustomed to an occasional spectator, and were not as easily spooked. Every evening we had a ringside seat to watch for V-shaped paths on the pond surface. Now and then a large blunt head with short ears cruised silently across the water. Each beaver clenched an aspen branch behind big orange teeth.

Near the lodge, I watched three little beavers swimming together. Why are the young of any species so much more appealing than their parents? Is it their bumbling innocence? The beaver kits were less than half grown. One swam to within six feet of me and I could plainly see the cross-check pattern on its stubby tail. The dark sky must have fooled them into activity earlier than usual. In another six weeks, the beaver family would be at home in their lodge, safe and snug from winter's icy blasts.

Beavers have no up-and-down cycles of abundance as do other rodents, such as rabbits. In watery Minnesota, the average litter size is five, but elsewhere, litters average three or four kits. The young are born late in the spring, fully furred, eyes open. The one-pound kits arrive with teeth already cut. Adult beavers are not vocal, but the kits will whine for attention. Once when I put my ear to the lodge, I could hear the little beavers whimpering inside. They sounded like tiny puppies.

When the lodge gets too crowded, the monogamous parents force their grown-up offspring to migrate. Tagged beavers have traveled anywhere from 25 to 150 miles to find new habitat.

As our clan multiplied, they constructed more dams and raised them higher to increase water reserve. To beavers, the buildup and maintenance of dams is a never-ending process.

The growing beaver family soon built a second lodge on the bank of the deep pond, across from the original. Or was it just an "insurance access," a passage of escape if the ice became too thick? Beavers sometimes run out of food before spring arrives. If their pantry is bare (or if the weather turns very mild), they will come out to eat fresh bark. And beavers that live in rivers or on lakeshores simply take up residence in the banks.

By early October, beavers had flooded the west side of the island. No wonder we heard mallards sounding off over there every morning. Most of the island became waterlogged because the aquatic engineers had built a lodge at the south end. Almost all of the timber was drowned, but I couldn't claim any great loss in lumber value. We capitalized on the dead trees for firewood, and those left standing made good den trees for birds and animals.

A good supply of aspen branches filled the water in front of lodge number four on the round pond, and in the natural pond downstream, they had raised the water level with yet another dam.

Two carefree young beavers swam by in front of me. At this rate, the toothy woodcutters were going to overdo a good thing and exhaust their food supply.

Most of the alder and aspen disappeared on the camp side of the first two ponds. It gave us an open view, but left enough scattered oaks and other trees for a windbreak. Popple was being thinned on the garden side of the wild hay meadow, too. Pointed stumps of white aspen formed clusters of short spears along the waterway.

When I look at the number of trees that beavers hang up, I'm convinced of one thing: The felling of trees is a hit-or-miss proposition with them. But even though they are night workers, very seldom do beavers make a fatal mistake with a falling tree.

Who ever heard of a lazy beaver? I found a perfect example of an unfinished beaver cut on a standing tree. The animal probably quit gnawing on that tree because of some real or imagined threat. I sawed off the five-inch aspen above the beaver's handiwork, and then severed the tooth-sculpted stump at ground level. It resembled an hourglass, with evenly spaced teeth marks all the way around; now it stands in my studio as a memento.

When most of this country was wilderness, fortunes were made in beaver pelts. Trappers could trade twelve skins for a rifle; one skin was barter for a pound of tobacco. And beaver meat furnished many a hearty meal for the early settlers. Both Indians and Europeans had great faith in beaver castoreum. This fluid was popular as a medical sedative, and is still used in the manufacture of perfume.

By 1900, due to unlimited trapping and netting, beavers were near extinction. In recent years, they have made a remarkable comeback—to the point of becoming a nuisance in some areas. Licensed trappers help to keep them in check. Also, some animals are live-trapped by state and local authorities for transport to remote waterways.

The industrious beaver is the only animal that manipulates the environment to suit its purpose. It is not belligerent unless attacked. And although a beaver's eyesight is poor, it has superb senses of hearing, smell, and touch.

Natural enemies of beavers accomplish very little culling in the wild. The coyote, fox, bobcat, lynx, or bear—and occasionally the great horned owl—can rarely surprise a beaver on land; if they do, it is most often a young animal. Only an otter can kill a beaver underwater.

Not everyone finds beavers as fascinating as I do. Game managers have to deal with complaints from irate landowners who are plagued by beaver damage—flooded roads or fields and ravaged trees. It all boils down to concern for money versus the natural order of things.

Beavers *can* put people in hot water, and sometimes it takes a lawsuit to settle a case of beaver damage. Not long ago, a Minnesota farm couple was hailed into court for refusing to lower the water level of a beaver pond. The dam, built across their marsh, was flooding part of a neighbor's field. The neighbor sued for "loss of use of our property." The defendants denied responsibility for the actions of a wild animal, and they refused to destroy the beaver dam. That prompted the district court judge to rule them in contempt:

"Thirty days in jail," he stormed, "unless you lower the water." The couple went to the state supreme court for a stay of sentence; at last report, the outcome was still uncertain.

Road access to our inland woods has always been a guessing game because of the beaver-flooded island. One day last winter when I mentioned beavers to a visiting firewood prospect from the area, he snapped: "Isn't anybody trapping 'em?"

Most (though not all) northwoods residents assume an adversary role concerning wild animals. Anything on four legs that threatens human status as conquerors of the land must be eliminated. It never occurred to this man that I *did not want* the beavers wiped out of the territory.

After his pickup rattled down the road, I thought, "If it weren't for beavers, both he and I might still be cramped into living space on the east coast . . ."

These docile furbearing vegetarians proved instrumental to the pioneering of America's vast wilderness. Searching for choice beaver streams, French voyageurs and other adventurers mapped trails across early America and Canada, opening new travel routes through the unsettled land. Beaver trappers were the first to exalt Yellowstone's geysers, and first to discover passes through the Rocky Mountains.

At the office one day during our initial exhilaration over the beavers' arrival, I raved about the event to one of my cohorts. My glowing account fell on deaf ears. This was her terse comment: "I can't get very excited about *rodents*."

To each his (or her) own. Although the mongrel she adores has no known historic lineage, the odd canine conglomeration must bring her comfort. (At least he is not a *rodent*.)

I concluded that people and their pets are not to be tampered with, and I'd best keep my interest in beavers to myself.

What good are beavers nowadays? Beaver-made ponds are very helpful in controlling spring runoff, and the water held back is beneficial to fish, waterfowl, and mammals large or small.

And yet, nothing lasts forever, including beaver ponds. When the ready supply of aspen is depleted, the beavers are forced to move on. The ponds dry up, and in a few years a lush green meadow replaces

51

the water area. Over the long haul, trees march in to take control, and the cycle continues.

7 A Permanent Shelter

Where we love is home,
Home that our feet may leave, but not our hearts."
Oliver Wendell Holmes

We were grilling hamburgers when a rain shower nearly doused the campfire. The tent hadn't been pitched yet, and the car was too far away for us to watch the burgers from there. Gail and I scrambled to cut four stakes from popple saplings, and pounded them into the ground around the fire. Then we balanced a big sheet of plywood across the stake tops and ducked out of the rain. The worst blew over, and the campfire lasted long enough to serve its purpose.

But a steady drizzle came in from the southwest, and we were compelled to sleep in the 'wagon that night.

"We need a *cabin*," the siblings informed me.

On each trip, the autumn nights grew colder, until we gave up tenting altogether. Sometimes our station wagon windows were covered with frost by morning. The idea of a cabin gathered momentum.

Late in October, I made Stan's acquaintance at Tomahawk Lake, ten miles away; he rented cabins during deer season. Before leaving his place, I bought a fifty-five gallon steel drum for $2.00—a cart-before-the-horse situation. When the time came, I'd make a barrel stove for our cabin.

The boys and I hacked out more brush and small trees to make room for a seasonal shelter. That evening we drove up the dark and deserted road to see if Jeff's empty cabin would be usable for hunters in November. Flashlight in hand, we examined the hollow building. It was closer to the 80 than Stan's, but it had no stove for use during deer season.

The trip up there was not a total loss. Seven-year-old Alan had brought along his buddy Kevin, and I parked on a hilltop where the three of us could study the sky full of sparkling stars. Suddenly the *northern lights* began to rotate! The two boys were completely awestruck. Never having seen such a phenomenon, they had more questions than I could answer. Kevin seemed to be especially taken aback. He gazed open mouthed at the wide-screen sky of aurora borealis, and in a voice tinged with fear, the boy gasped, "Maybe it's God coming!"

*　　　*　　　*

Another year passed before I could start construction. During that time we scrounged used lumber from throwaways around home. (Our cabin project was scaled to low overhead.) We certainly kept the neighborhood clean. Down the block, a friend's discarded picket fence made an important contribution of pine boards. When a neighbor replaced his front door, we gladly accepted the reject, because it had three small windows. Another neighbor's outgrown treehouse produced handy sheets of half-inch plywood, and so on.

It is amazing how much useful lumber is tossed out by people in just one block of suburbia. Nationwide, it must total millions of board feet annually. And at today's lumber prices, we weren't fussy. Even a roll of unused tarpaper turned up, along with a battered downspout. Our shameless scavenging embarrassed Miriam, but the boys and I had a goal.

By summer's end, we had an impressive pile of scrap boards in the camp clearing. And from an abandoned house up the road, we salvaged a door with frame. The owner said: "Take anything, but leave the outhouse."

October 1

The woods glowed with October gold when I pulled up to begin work on a cabin. Alone this time, I looked forward to a week's vacation dedicated to carpentry.

At the lumberyard in Larsville, I had selected fourteen-foot fir rafters, indispensable to a cabin's roof; nobody ever threw away anything *that* long. When I paid the bill, I felt all the more pleased at our pile of free boards.

As I unloaded lumber and camp gear, the sky turned gray and a cool wind blew in from the northwest. If only the weather would hold for the next few days.

Before starting on construction, I went over to examine the beaver lodge. Not that I planned to plagiarize their architectural style—I just wanted to see how much they had improved the dome-shaped hut of sticks and mud. By now it stood five feet above ground level, and wide, skidding beaver tracks marked gooey clay daubed over the lodge.

When I crossed the high ground between ponds, a dozen mallards quacked alarm and took flight. Following the contours of the dam made for easier walking, and raccoon footprints were plentiful at waterline.

Out on the tip of the island, I paused to admire the beavers' handiwork. A sudden squall of sleet crackled down through the trees, and a flurry of yellow leaves descended. Tapioca-size beads of ice pelted my face until I leaned against the leeward side of a big ash trunk. The eerie beauty of the ice storm lasted but a minute or two, as if Mother Nature meant only to award me a brief demonstration of her versatility.

That evening I cooked supper on a campstove; though never as much fun as a campfire, it did save time. Just about dark, a flock of bluebills whistled in low over the ponds. As a rule, these migrants signal the end of the duck season. They were early. This was opening day for waterfowl.

By 9:00 P.M., I crawled into the sleeping bag in the station wagon.
October 2
Up at daylight; frost covered the car. Three grouse flew in from the road after a first course of gravel for breakfast. At pond's edge, a mink bounded through the weeds twenty feet from me. His dark brown fur looked prime.

When the sun came up, I took my twelve-guage and dropped two mallards for a future duck dinner. One of my hip boots leaked, and I got a wet foot in the bargain. After field dressing the ducks, I set the innards down in the weeds where prowlers could clean up the mess overnight.

Thanks to nephew Tommy, we had a "cooler" in camp for food storage. That boy had a passion for digging into the ground. Armed with a pickaxe and spade, he would be formidable competition for a badger. Tommy had fashioned a "well"—a two-foot-deep hole—to keep our perishables fresh in warm weather. Inside the hole, a deep metal pail with a lid kept out mud and debris—and scavengers. The cooler-pit also gave us an indication of moisture in the surrounding soil, during spring thaw or after heavy rains, it filled with water. In summer, the temperature underground held consistently to the low forties. On the warmest days, we put a chunk of ice in the bottom of the pail, but that wouldn't be necessary at this time of year.

I plopped the mallards into the makeshift refrigerator and placed a wide board across the top, anchored by a heavy rock to discourage marauders.

A steady wind blew from the south. The overnight frost soon melted away, and a thin layer of ice on the jugs of water kept them cool.

Working alone, I made slow progress. I sorted boards and set up two sawhorses to cut a maple and birch tree for roof supports across the front and back.

October 3

Clear weather continued. A grouse flew by as I cooked breakfast. He seemed to favor my camp clearing.

By noon I had dug a shallow trench for the oak-log floor supports on all four sides, and squared the foundation corners. Buried fieldstones prolonged my efforts, but they added color and character to the fireplace circle.

At the base of each corner post, I made a tarpaper form to hold cement. It took two ninety-pound bags of mix, with water carried from the ponds. Wet cement around each post base gave them an air of permanence. After it cured, the cement would be a firm support and also ward off ground decay.

High overhead, a flock of Canadian honkers winged southward in a shifting V-shape against the blue. The sound of their social music faded in and out of the winds at that altitude. And once a flight of snow geese streamed over, flashing white in the sun. The haunting call of wild geese in autumn skies tantalized me as I worked.

In the afternoon, a curious chipmunk paid me a visit. He scampered around me at first, then boldly ran up take a light nibble at my boot tip. I tossed out a few bread crumbs and other goodies. No camp is complete without a cheerful "chippie" to keep you company.

October 4

By the time Tommy and my son Alan arrived, solid 4 x 4 floorboard supports were in position. After four days alone, it was nice to have company again—especially helpers. I squared ends of picket fence boards while the boys hammered on the floor.

Before we nailed down the last floorboard, I scattered mothballs on the ground underneath to discourage strange dwellers. Jeff, up the road, had given me serious advice: "I'd build it well off the ground, to keep skunks out." I considered that, but gambled on buried oak logs trenched with fieldstones for the base—and mothballs.

The floor was in place by sundown, and we felt quite satisfied with ourselves. In spite of October's frosty nights, the boys elected to sleep in the tent, but off the ground on the new cabin floor. With a borrowed tent heater, they assured me, "We'll be as warm as toast."

October 5

When I crawled out of the car to head for the camp clearing, Tommy and Alan already had a bonfire going.

"Almost froze to death," they groaned. "That stupid heater only lasted about four hours!"

The teakettle soon hissed to a boil. A hot cup of chocolate and a bowl of cereal improved their outlook.

We hoisted two fourteen-foot 2 x 4s into position for front and back roof ends. And for extra strength, we added a five-inch-thick birch pole across the front. The bark had to be peeled off first, or the birch would rot. At the lower, back end, we used a maple pole along with the horizontal 2 x 4.

The cabin began to take shape at last. Reluctantly, the boys left for home after supper (school tomorrow), and I was on my own again.

October 6

Another in a string of gorgeous days.

Over by the garden, I checked the apple trees, a Wealthy and a Haralson, which needed protection from winter hazards. I stretched tree wrap around each one's slender trunk near the ground to ward

59

off mice, and placed a circle of wire mesh fence around them to discourage deer and snowshoe hares.

I also fenced in a small tamarack planted in a southern exposure where it could soak up sunlight. The young transplant's delicate needles had already turned to a soft gold; before long it would be bare, since the tamarack is the only conifer that sheds its needles.

My tomato plants were black from frost, but the green-topped carrots were healthy. I pulled one up for a tasty reward. It was high time to dig the carrots and parsnips before they froze in the ground.

A strong wind blew all day. I separated the aluminum extension ladder to use half of it at each roof end, because it saved time. During the afternoon, a sudden gust of wind blew down the ladder while I stood below. The sharper end very narrowly missed my head. I drew a thankful breath and sat down to weigh the dangers of working alone. The ladder might have cut open my face, or broken my glasses, and sent me off to a doctor. After that, I anchored the top of the ladder on windy days.

When I nailed up the last rafter, I could visualize a small cabin. But after six continuous days on this labor of love, it was time to shift gears and return to the city.

On the way, I stopped at the sawmill. They stocked a choice of rough-cut lumber; oak, elm, popple, or pine. Rates were about half of lumberyard prices, and I chose popple. It is easy to nail into, and if properly dried, will not warp or rot abnormally—unless it is in contact with the ground. The boards would be ready for me on my next trip.

*　　　*　　　*

Back again in mid-October, we stopped first at Tomahawk Lake to assemble the stove kit. Stan cut openings in the steel drum with his saber saw. It took awhile to fasten the iron door and chimney collar to the drum, but finally our barrel stove was ready for use.

"Not quite," Stan said. "Let's light some kindling in it to burn off the paint."

We moved the stove into his farmyard, away from the buildings, and lit the fire. Blue paint bubbled and cooked on the metal surface, and some kind of chemical residue smoldered on the inside. The burning paint smelled terrible. We'd have to haul the stove up to the 80 another day.

Getting to work on our cabin, the boys and I placed a white oak center beam under the roof's fir rafters. Only the biggest spikes would penetrate it.

"That thing will hold an elephant," Tommy proclaimed.

In the afternoon, the Lindstrom brothers came over to peruse our new structure. They told us about their recently completed cabin, a half mile in from the gravel road. I had not seen it yet, and just as well—it spared me the embarrassment of comparison.

"Whatya gonna use fer a stove?" they wondered.

I told them about the barrel stove we had in the works. Oscar said he had a barrel stove too, and continued, "Did you ever see that camper bus up the road, set back in the trees? We used to bunk in it during deer season. Well, one year we came up from the cities, night before deer opener. Cold night. Somebody'd busted off the padlock and stole our stove! Hadda drive all the way back to St. Paul to get another one that night. Sure didn't get much sleep before it was time to get up and go huntin'."

"At least your new cabin is back farther, out of sight of the road. Should be safer," I offered. In our case, we'd just have to take our chances.

"Ya," they continued, "but last week a bear broke in . . . he took a down-filled sleeping bag—best one we had—out in the woods and just shredded it all to pieces."

The brothers laughed about it, but I could tell they'd like to get that bear in their rifle sights during deer season. (Minnesota's black bear had not yet been elevated to the class of protected game animal.)

Toward the end of October, we toiled another weekend on the cabin. This time we picked up the barrel stove at Stan's and ceremoniously carried it into camp. But setting it up would have to wait.

Meanwhile, we thought it necessary to camouflage the stove while we were gone. As we had learned from the Lindstroms, this kind of heating apparatus is very popular in the north country, and we didn't want it to "walk away." In the brush at the edge of the wild hay meadow, we carefully covered it with weeds and branches.

As a further precaution against theft, I had previously marked the sliding iron air vent with my name, using one of those electric devices that punches a series of depressions into metal. I also tapped a secret code number into an obscure place on the stove.

Our barrel stove parts came from an estate sale, a steal at $5.00, even though I had to hammer off the rusty bolts with a cold chisel. The day I carried that box of heavy iron stove parts downtown on the bus didn't gain me any points in popularity. As the bus filled up, I was pressured into moving it off the seat beside me. Then people had to trip over the box in the aisle until I struggled off the bus.

This may sound like more trouble than it was worth, but at the old general store in Larsville, barrel stove hardware sold for over $40.00—and fifty-five gallon drums went as high as $14.00 each. Excluding labor, my total stove cost was a mere $7.00 without stovepipe. Once hooked on a bargain, I'm reluctant to surrender.

Roll roofing came next. The sun had softened the quarter-inch-thick material, making it easier to uncurl. I climbed up with a pail of roofing nails to clinch down the first strip at the lower end. Each succeeding section would overlap.

The flat roof sloped from nine feet high at the front to seven feet off the ground at the back. It gave me an elevated view of the ponds, and before lifting up another heavy strip of roofing, I paused to take in the scene.

A lone marsh hawk patrolled the slough. I envied his effortless shifting and soaring on the wind, a living example of "free as a bird." None of *his* time need be spent building a shelter; his plumage took care of that. The same applied to clothing. Once a year at molting time, the hawk could count on a new suit, always in fashion and never a feather changed in design. Paris could pull no strings to alter his style. Only the unending quest for food concerned him, and the gliding bird looked totally content with his pursuits.

Three hours later my knees were sore and the roof was done. I stood up and drew in a deep breath of satisfaction.

The next phase would be the inside front wall, to be covered with squared-off picket fence boards. While I cut pine slats to uniform length, young Alan hammered away. Once he stopped pounding to solemnly declare: "This cabin sure is made out of hard work."

So far, the building had no siding. By Sunday night we had fastened a ten-foot roll of heavy plastic over all four walls. At least that would keep out the rain or snow until we applied siding. Darkness came too soon, and I was hitting my thumb more often than nails. We headed for home.

On the next trip, Tommy and I unveiled the hidden stove and carried it into the cabin. The natives had warned me that a barrel stove needs four or five inches of sand in the bottom to avoid burning through, so I poured in sand and leveled it off.

Two stovepipe elbows were enough, one inside and one out. I decided not to cut a hole in the roof, sending the stovepipe straight up, because that offered more chance for a roof leak. (As it turned out, a jog in the piping helped to slow down the draft speed.)

It took some jostling to get the pipes into a firm fit. Then I climbed onto the roof to set on the spark arrester cap, and to position guide wires for steadying the chimney. It wouldn't do to have the chimney blow off sometime in the middle of the night.

From below, Tommy and I studied the cartoon-type chimney, grinned, and proclaimed it a "hillbilly shack."

As a fire precaution, we placed an aluminum "thimble" with airspace around the stovepipe where it left the shack. And inside and out, we stapled asbestos paper on the wall around the piping. On the wall behind the stove, we used heavy sheets of asbestos.

By now, we were chomping at the bit to build a fire and test the stove. But it was already late afternoon, time to try deer hunting during the best hours. It wouldn't be wise to leave a fire in the stove this first time while we were off in the woods.

No venison turned up by sundown, and Tommy had to leave for the city. Cars full of weekend hunters rattled gravel on the road for awhile, and then the woods were dark and quiet.

I lifted the globe on the kerosene lantern, and for lack of a scissors, trimmed the wick with a tin shears. If left uneven, the wick burned dimmer and gave off excess smoke to blacken the glass. I touched a match to the wick and lowered the globe. "Let there be light." I hung the old lantern on a rafter nail, and decided it was short on illumination but long on nostalgia.

I pumped up the campstove to start supper and picked a stump for a table until shelves could be built. Before long, the tempting smell of frying hamburger permeated the shack.

Food first, then heat. The magic moment had arrived—time to light my first fire in the barrel stove! I opened the drafts and stuck a kindling teepee of pine slivers into the sand inside the stove. As a carryover from Boy Scout days, I vowed to light it with just one match. The tiny flame took hold and grew taller in devouring the resinous wood. Enough sweet-smelling pine smoke drifted out to perfume the air. I added dry sticks in graduating sizes until the fire showed sincerity, and the stove appeared to draw just fine. Within minutes, welcome heat filled the enclosure.

I expected a ridiculous heat loss; by no means was the building airtight, but that made it safer, after all. The way that barrel stove kicked out heat, too much oxygen could be consumed without adequate ventilation.

I stepped outside to look at the hillbilly chimney top. Smoke rolled forth in a steady stream, and sparks dissipated when they struck the lid cap. Tomorrow I might add a piece of screen up there for further protection. Even though the woods were damp this fall, I didn't want to be accused of starting a forest fire. Out there against the background of darkness, light from the lantern multiplied through the translucent plastic shell. People in any passing car would think I had built a greenhouse.

No one could know the pleasure I felt when I stepped back inside. Warmth radiated from the stove, and I glanced at the comforting pile of dry wood against the front wall. Even if the wind came up and the temperature dropped, this ramshackle shelter beat sleeping in a car or tent.

Along the wall opposite the stove, the folding cot and mattress looked inviting. I unrolled the sleeping bag, then poked up the fire. 7:30 was too early to turn in . . . might as well stretch out on the bed to relax in solid comfort.

I gazed up at the lantern. Kerosene fumes triggered memories of youth on the farm . . . those twice-daily chores of hand-milking Holsteins in a barn lit only by lanterns . . . the smell of hay, and cud-chewing cows . . . how my brother and I broke the monotony by squirting milk into the cats' mouths . . . and one severe winter when the thermometer outside the barn stalled at fifty-five degrees below zero.

The warm air made me drowsy. I got up to stoke the fire with heavier logs for the night, and smoke rolled out of the iron door. Clearly, I'd have to learn the barrel stove's eccentricities. Meanwhile, the solution was simple: open the shack's door to let smoke out and fresh air in—basic air-conditioning.

I turned down the lantern wick until it sputtered out, and the black night swallowed all sight and sound.

The invigorated fire made my cheeks flush. Now the air intake of the iron door permitted the only illumination. Yellow-orange light flickered and danced in miniature streaks of lightning against the inside of the white front door—mesmerizing. Long hours of labor blurred away in tranquility.

Along about 3:00 A.M., my nose got cold. I pulled an extra blanket over my face, knowing full well it wouldn't solve the problem. The fire had gone out. Either I could remain moderately comfortable for the time being—and risk freezing stiff as a board by morning—or I had to eject myself from the warm sleeping bag to jack up the fire.

Oh, that floor was cold! (Solid, though.) I reached for my flashlight and threw down an old coat for a rug.

Inside the barrel, a half-burned log held enough coals to prolong the fire. Ten minutes later—blessed with an over-supply of heat again—I crawled back in for another four hours' rest.

Daylight came, and I had survived my first night in the new shelter. I clanked open the stove door and jostled the remaining coals. Pine-board scraps soon flamed and crackled to conquer the morning chill.

I pushed open the shack door. Woodsmoke trailed from the chimney, and a wispy layer of blue haze floated over the slough. Exhilarating. A grand place to greet Monday morning, far from the freeways.

When the black and battered teakettle wheezed into boiling, I poured a cup of coffee. Ah-h . . . the simple life! I was king for a day.

8 Around Camp

We're tenting tonight on the old campground,
Give us a song to cheer
Our weary hearts, a song of home
And friends we love so dear.
Walter Kittredge

Something had bitten or clawed an eight-inch hole in the plastic wall of the shack. A curious 'coon? Stray dog? Most of the inside walls were covered with a hodge podge of boards by this time, and the plastic served only as a weatherproofing windbreak. We always hooked the door, but never bothered with a padlock. If you locked the door on a seasonal dwelling, thieves or vandals suspected you of hiding something valuable; then they were inclined to kick down the door.

Lack of normal rainfall left the ponds pitifully low that summer. Animal and bird tracks told the story of our ponds' popularity—deer, raccoons, mink, herons, and assorted birds left their footprints around the edges. The water impoundment became a lifesaving oasis for wildlife.

The boys helped carry water to the thirsty young trees transplanted around camp—several spruce and pines, five small cedars, and two walnut trees. With the ponds so low, it was like robbing Peter to pay Paul. But the transplants didn't stand a chance otherwise, and in a few weeks the ground would freeze. One good rain before then could bring salvation.

A new kind of track appeared in our entrance road to the ponds. Someone had ridden a horse out to the island and back. It reminded me of Robert Frost's poem:

> *Whose woods these are I think I know.*
> *His house is in the village though;*
> *He will not see me stopping here . . .*

Never had the water dropped so far, and we worried about the beavers' surviving winter if it didn't rain before freeze-up. Even the deepest pond held scarcely enough water to store their winter supply of aspen limbs. Dry beaver trenches were exposed to the sun; now we could trace their channels.

Beside the "deep pond," tracks preserved in dried mud indicated a herd of cattle had made a desperate stop for a drink. A local farmer must have been moving his cows down the road to new pasture. The natural pond farthest south in the slough had dried up completely, and a cracked mosaic of hardened gray dirt displayed fissures two inches deep.

*　　　*　　　*

The shack door needed a window. Although light came through the temporary plastic walls, it was impossible to see more than blurred shapes outside. To avoid the problem of breakage with glass, I used quarter-inch Plexiglas. A few brads nailed into strips of moulding held the two square feet of clear material in place. Now we could look out at the wild hay meadow without opening the door, even in winter, because Plexiglas won't frost up like glass.

In the other front corner facing south, a streak of light came through a hole near the bottom of the "retired" door. There had been no hole there before. It looked like a bullet hole, entering the shack from the outside. We tried to line it up with something inside, but failed to find any point of impact to coincide with its path. It remained a mystery to us, and we didn't like the implications.

Between camp and the road, a mature basswood became my next project. The sixteen-inch trunk showed decay, so why not sacrifice the old tree to let the cluster's young trees grow faster? The chain saw made short work of the soft white wood. We dragged a five-foot section over and dug a hole to stand it in. On top of this we placed the round flat half of a discarded cable spool. The three-foot circle of weathered boards made a rustic camp table.

For chairs, plain stumps suited us. *Anything* to sit on looked good by this time. Then I decided to make a simple *Kubbestuhl*.* Nothing

*Pronounced koob-eh-stool, a Norwegian chair, often enhanced by hand-carved designs or brightly painted in rosemaling.

fancy. I selected a choice part of the basswood trunk about three feet long—one with a natural curve—and chain-sawed half way through at the center. From the top, I cut down *with the woodgrain* to remove a quarter of the log. When finished, I notched the back at the top and leaned it against a small oak for the most comfortable chair in camp.

Little by little, we enlarged the pulloff clearing for parking the car. Every foot advanced toward the shack saved us walking distance for carrying gear. No matter how much paraphernalia we might haul in from the road, something we needed was "out in the car"— another hundred-yard trip for one of us.

An obstinate stump required use of an axe, a spade, and a grubhoe—and lots of sweat—before those roots would surrender. When victory finally came, we leveled off the hole and sat down to rest. Thereafter we could back the car in a little closer.

The boys wandered off to explore, and I started on a frame for a window. Our only daylight came from the south side door, and it would be nice to look out east toward the road. Plexiglas would be fine here, too. After hammering in the last nail, I stepped inside to admire the view.

The boys came romping down the road and charged into camp, starved. Neither of them saw the new window as such a big deal, at least not on an empty stomach.

We took advantage of midsummer's bounty by roasting corn on the cob over a campfire, with the husks left on to hold in moisture. The ears won't scorch if they are turned often above the coals, and the tender sweet corn gains a delightful smoky flavor, far superior to corn boiled in water. I prefer this roasting method to wrapping the complete ear of corn in mud before baking in the coals, Indian-style. For dessert, we picked and ate wild raspberries by the handful.

Mosquito nets were a must at night in July and August. I hadn't used one since the jungles of New Guinea. We rigged ropes from the ceiling and draped a net over each bed to foil the flying pests.

After dark, I sat transfixed by the campfire, and the boys had fun trying to capture lightning bugs in the slough grass. A few "glow worms," trapped by their mating signal lights, ended up in a glass jar for study.

A coyote howled just before daybreak, and I stayed awake until dawn. When I opened my eyes again, a soft ray of sunlight probed in through the new window. I got up to enjoy my first sunrise from *inside* the shack. No other window ever gave me more satisfaction.

This would be another day for home improvement. Any dwelling needs endless care, and the shack was not immune. As they say, it's the little things that make a house a home.

I built a shelf above the campstove counter, and put up two tin breadboxes to foil the mice. Then it was time to air out the mattresses and replace one—mice and the little red squirrel had made it useless for us. I plugged a hole in the corner of the shack where the squirrel had gnawed an entrance.

Another camp table out front would come in handy. Our rustic round table didn't hold everything that should be kept off the ground. With leftover picket fence boards and tools at hand, I could once again presume to be a carpenter.

Whatever I may lack in construction skills, I make up for with inventive approach. "One-of-a-kind" best describes my technique in carpentry. There were no building codes here to stifle my creativity—witness the shack.

Halfway through my project, it occurred to me that a four-foot table wasted a lot of space underneath. After nailing on the top boards, I added a shelf below to give the table more stability. Only then did I realize I had built a table *and woodbox* combination, within easy reach of the front (and only) door—a very satisfying (and surprising) accomplishment.

Before I lost my constructive momentum, I patched up some holes in the shack, and built a shelf inside for the portable cookstove. Any trifling improvement brings satisfaction to the simple life of a backwoodsman.

Some of my urban friends could never understand my sojourns to the wild woods. Being out of touch with the pioneer life, they failed to consider the amount of time needed to perform basic chores, and they often asked: "What do you *do* up there in the brush all the time?" These people looked bewildered when I told them I could never keep up with things I wanted to do on the wild 80.

*   *   *

On a warm October day, the heady smells of autumn filled the woods. An overcast sky threatened rain, and sound carried well on the moisture-laden air. Once I heard the long and lonely hoot of an owl, muted by distance. And from my camp chair, I listened to two frogs as they carried on an argument on either side of me. In this mild and misty atmosphere, they might have been debating whether it was spring or fall.

By this time, rainfall had replenished the ponds, and beaver activity had accelerated. Aspen branches were piled high in the deepest pond beside their lodge.

I walked down the road to see what might be done about a big tree the beavers had dropped on the power line. The electric wire sagged precariously. I was standing on soggy ground, holding a chainsaw . . . No thanks—the risk wasn't worth it. I left the tree for maintenance crew removal. (A few days later, the wind solved the problem.)

Just twenty yards in from the gravel road, a dead ash looked good for fireplace wood. Also, I planned to saw off four-inch-thick slabs to be used as a walkway in my back yard at home.

The tree had drowned from beaver backup, and it now stood gray and dry. Big sections of bark hung loose on its eighteen-inch-thick trunk. Before putting the chain saw to it, I peeled off a wide chunk of bark to better plan my notch cut. If I could direct the tree to fall *toward* the road, I'd have fewer steps to haul the heavy wood.

About three feet above the tree's base, between the dried bark and solid wood, I found a complete snakeskin. It had been a small snake, probably a red-bellied—not known as a tree climber. But at shedding time, the reptile had picked an excellent place to accomplish its "off with the old skin, on with the new."

I stared toward Swens's woods, and couldn't believe my eyes—not one, but *five bluebirds* on the fence along the road. I hadn't seen any of their kind for years. It must have been a migrating family. I wanted to tell the rare birds to take note of the bluebird houses posted nearby—and be sure to come back in the spring.

Peace and quiet settled on the marsh. At dusk I went down to the ponds, and a hen mallard quacked in alarm as she lifted off the water. A circle of widening ripples reflected the waning light. Far back in the woods, the owls began a hooting duel.

The pile of dry wood inside the shack was reassuring; a few pine slivers and a strip of birchbark were soon ablaze in the barrel stove. (I have a weakness for the perfume of burning birchbark; its tangy fragrance is the very essence of northern woods.) Darkness came earlier now, and the fire felt good again.

I lit the kerosene lantern and hung it from a rafter. Because my campstove was obscured by a shadow cast by the lantern, I needed a flashlight to see if anything was burning while I cooked supper. The modern gas lantern had spoiled me, and next time I would bring it along.

By eight o'clock, the full moon dodged purple clouds, and it put the ducks into a cheery mood. Those mallards behind the island could not get everything discussed during the day.

The bugs and insects were gone, except for a solitary moth that found new life from the warm stove. After I shut off the lantern, the moth stopped fluttering against the glass.

I stretched out on the top bunk and listened to the patter of tiny feet across the roof. Beneath the campstove shelf, a mouse rattled paper in the safety of darkness. Mice were multiplying in the absence of a resident weasel.

During the night, a beaver dropped a tree now and then. And once I woke up when a barred owl hooted close by: "Hooh, hooh, hoo-hoo . . . hooh, hooh, hoo-hooooo . . ." The last note trailed off in a gutteral slur. Evidently the owl had chosen a perch in the big elm out front for a good view of the wild hay meadow and ponds. Any prowling mouse, weasel, rabbit, or muskrat—or for that matter, a fidgeting bird at roost—now entered a time of peril.

Moonlight broke through wind-driven clouds and fooled me with a false dawn. When I got up to stoke the fire, it was only 5:00 A.M. Back to the bunk for another hour or two.

Toward morning, coyotes howled again, setting off a farm dog's barking in the distance.

A light frost covered the ground, but the glorious sunrise promised a pleasant October day. From beyond the slough island, mallards greeted daylight with excited duck talk. Before the beavers came, the west side of the island had been all dry slough. Thanks to those industrious four-legged loggers, we could enjoy a wider variety of wildlife close to camp.

By now the trees were festooned in finery, with yellows, browns, reds, and maroons replacing the greens of summer. A few mallards lingered on the ponds, but most of the songbirds had departed. In a few weeks, the weasel and snowshoe would change to a coat of white in time to match the snow.

I set off to breathe in the fragrance of October woods and soak up some of the glory.

After I'd spent most of the day in the backwoods, my snacks were gone, and hunger pangs reminded me of an experiment I had in the works. That morning, while the fire blazed in the barrel stove, I had this brainstorm: why not separate some of the coals, set a small grill over them, wrap a potato in foil, and . . . I knew the fire would be out by now, but the potato ought to be done. It would give me a good start toward supper.

All the way back, I visualized that brown-skinned, steaming, mouth-watering potato, sliced down the middle, with a gob of yellow butter melting over mealy white; a little salt and pepper, a fork . . . even the chewy skin would be tasty. Most people scorn baked potato skins, but I find them very flavorsome, and they are also the most nutritious part.

At last I entered the shack; I could already taste that magnificent baked potato. The stove was cool, as expected, but I'd soon have the fire going again to warm up the spud if necessary.

I lifted the iron door and peeked inside the stove. Gingerly, I reached into the gray ashes for the crinkled ball of foil, and unwrapped the prize. It was "done" all right, clear through, burned to crisp charcoal. Just a teaspoonful of edible white remained on one side.

Indeed, my vision of a stylish meal in the shack had literally gone up in smoke. I surmised that a burning log must have shifted to tilt the grill, and my tantalizing tuber slid off into hot coals to a point of no return. I shoved the shack door open and gave the black potato a hefty fling into the weeds.

Before winter paralyzed the land, certain chores needed tending to. I set the folding bed outside the shack and added sheets of plywood over the flooring of picket fence boards to give the floor more solidity. First, though, I pulled up a floor board and threw down a handful of mothballs to discourage skunks. In the fall these animals search out winter dens, often choosing the underside of a building. One irritated skunk could render the shack uninhabitable for months.

Road traffic increased at this time of year. Grouse hunters cruised the side roads looking for unposted woods, and deer hunters were doing advance scouting. Seven or eight cars passed by during the day—heavy activity for this locale.

The little red squirrel had rebuilt a nest above the inside rafters. Furthermore, the rapscallion had eaten or carted off all of the unhusked walnuts I was saving to plant. Time would tell if he was a better planter.

I was in for a surprise when I reached for an old pair of hip boots that I'd left hanging in the shack. One boot seemed heavier than the other, and the foot part felt solid. When I rolled down the top half to look inside, I found the boot packed ankle-high with acorns! The self-invited squirrel had found the perfect place for his winter pantry.

On a previous visit, the boys had left a trap set in the slag pile, trying to catch a woodchuck, and they had forgotten to retrieve it. While I worked on the flooring, I heard the tinkle of a bell—the trap was rigged to give warning if something was captured. The red squirrel had one foot in the clamp. When I released him, he scampered up the big elm tree, proving he was still highly mobile.

Around four in the afternoon, black clouds rolled in, and the darkened sky triggered the owls into a hooting frenzy. Even in daylight, the haunting call of an owl in the woods puts me in touch with primeval mysteries.

When the sun burst through once more, the owls went quiet. I started up the chain saw, and a flock of startled mallards arose from the ponds to circle the island. They came back by sundown, drifting in to calm waters for the night.

9 Winter Moods

The summer hath his joys,
And winter his delights . . .
Thomas Campion

When I stepped from the car on a crisp December night, the silence was overwhelming—a world apart from the one I had just left. Moonlight filtered through the trees to form a tangled mesh of shadows on the snow. The shack's vinyl shell glistened in the eerie light, and nothing stirred.

I unhooked the door and went in to light the kerosene lantern. Everything remained as I had left it—of most importance, the barrel stove. Now for a comforting fire.

I missed having the boys along this time. Earlier that month, Alan and Nathan had their first chance to wallow in the shack's coziness. They called it "neat." I accepted their misuse of the word, realizing that the dictionary definition of *neat* would never quite describe our shack: "Brilliant, elegant, clean, pure, undiluted, tasteful, free from bungling [?], orderly, tidy, *compactness* [that one I might swallow] and . . . jauntiness in appearance."

Whatever the boys meant by "neat," and no matter how much they enjoyed the shack, neither of them stirred from his sleeping bag cocoon in the middle of the night. When the fire died down, I had to be the hero.

I suppose part of a boy's camping fun comes from his chance to shake off the inhibitions of society. Males of any age need a retreat from the niceties of cultured life, an escape from encumbering rules and regulations. For instance, the boys made great sport of filling their mouths with water and spewing it onto the hot barrel stove. That loud sizzle and rising cloud of steam fascinated them. Such outlandish behavior opened a whole new world away from their mother's apron strings. The lads would have their share of regimentation soon enough. To quote Ben Franklin: "A little nonsense now and then is relished by the best of men."

As an example of our loose living at the shack, when we had to hang up something—wet socks, or an extra cooking pan—we just reached for the hammer and nails.

By lantern light, I made these notes for the day: "Alone in the shack on a Saturday night, I mull over the contrast to life back in the city. Down there tonight, a multitude of urbanites are pursuing the ritual of doing the town. Crowds of people are unwinding on the weekend, packing the taverns and dancehalls to fill their lungs with stale air and tobacco smoke. Up here I'm spared the noise of blaring bands that rely more on volume than on musical talent. Nothing here in the woods assaults my eardrums. Only the crackle of popple logs in the barrel stove interrupts my reverie; and I don't mind a whiff of woodsmoke.

"Occasionally on this frigid night, a tree in the forest pops like a rifle shot in the cold. The teakettle hisses forth vapors, humidifying the air as it comes to a boil. In the dim glow of the lantern, I squint again at a sign nailed to the wall beside the door. With a wood-burnishing tool, young Alan had inscribed on a slab of pine board: 'Home Away From Home.' That says it all.

"Primitive it is, but the shack underscores man's basic need for protection from the elements. Even the cavemen caught on to that. Whether it's a cold winter night, or a summer downpour, it feels great to be inside.

"In this rustic retreat, cost of fuel is measured only in muscle power—energy expended in chain-sawing, splitting, and carrying firewood. No monthly heating bill plagues me here.

"As I stretch out on the top bunk, my eyes rove the shack's interior, and I muse: This 'carpenter's nightmare' is constructed of a variety of woods, anything available—fir beams, burr oak corner posts cut on the site, white oak crossbeam, aspen and red oak vertical studs, popple roof boards, and pine slats for floorboards, plus odd pieces of plywood panels.

"The whole structure probably cost less than $200, and before long it will pay for itself in avoidance of motel rent."

During the night, I awoke to the howling of coyotes ("brush wolves" as the natives like to call them). Having seen their tracks at times, I knew there were some around. The "yap-yap-yap—ow-oo-ooo . . ." warbled off at the end, as the wily predator communicated his position to the others. After a short pause, another coyote answered from afar. Their howls carried well on the crisp night air, and the thin plastic walls were no barrier to sound. Pleasantly primitive. My dreams might find me lost on the frozen Yukon . . . hungry wolves closing in . . .

Trees creaked from the cold in the morning, but the snap in the air made wood splitting easier.

Human footprints in the snow led toward the frozen ponds—a trespasser with small feet. No sign of traps on the shores.

I set out for the island to keep a promise. My friend Harley carves and paints lifelike duck decoys, and he prefers basswood. The soft white wood is firm and it takes paint or stain very well. I told him to sharpen his tools and I'd bring him a short log.

A basswood with a hole at the base assuaged my feeling about sacrificing an entire tree for such frivolous purpose. The trunk was fourteen inches thick, and a three-foot section would be enough for at least two carved decoys. The basswood took more than forty years to reach this size, and the chain saw brought it down in less than forty seconds. Two saw cuts above the hollow core gave me a solid log.

I huffed and puffed through snow and brush and cattails to drag it out to the road.

A wood duck house needed cleaning out, and I added fresh wood shavings to the nest. In the spring, water would back up to the oak's trunk, and any young ducklings should have an easy time of it. Baby wood ducks have been observed plummeting fifty feet to *pavement* with no ill effects.

That afternoon, two young men came into camp with a problem. Their car slid into a ditch a mile or so down the road, and they had another two miles to walk to meet some friends for snowmobiling. I drove them up to a rendezvous point with their buddies, where they would find plenty of help to extricate their car.

BUILDING A WILDERNESS RETREAT

*   *   *

In January, Alan found bear tracks in the snow on the island. An earlier thaw must have brought old bruin out of hibernation to scrounge for food. Evidently our shack did not tempt him, or the bear could easily have broken through the walls of plastic sheeting. We never left any edibles around to attract large scavengers.

The barrel stove kept Brian, Alan, and me comfortable, but around midnight a howling wind came out of the north to rattle the flimsy plastic walls. When I crawled out of bed to stoke the fire, I also stuffed rags into drafty holes.

A much colder day greeted us at dawn. A road-killed mink we'd found was frozen to the camp table.

After breakfast, the boys hiked over to the old log cabin behind the hermit's place. By the time they returned, I had secured the double bunk bed frame against the rear wall.

In the afternoon, while the boys thawed out from their hike, I pruned oak trees around camp. Winter is the best time to trim oaks. Pruning them in summer can encourage the spread of oak wilt, practically the only disease that can harm these sturdy trees.

*   *   *

Near the end of January, Gail and I took off for the wild 80 again. The snow always looked deeper up north. This time the gravel road had been plowed, but before parking the car, we had to shovel through the packed bank for a pulloff spot—just like our driveway at home.

Walking was an effort in two feet of snow. Carrying gear in to the shack warmed us up as we tromped a trench-path.

There was a deer bed beside the shack. I suspect that in choosing to rest so close to the road, the deer felt safer from brush wolves.

I tacked tarpaper strips over holes in the split plastic walls, and before long the shack held heat again. At dusk, the owls hooted a welcome from the hushed winter woods.

Morning arrived crisp and clear. Under the theory of "what you don't know can't hurt you," we never bothered with a thermometer.

80

After breakfast, I fueled up the chain saw to cut more firewood. To escape the noise, Gail hiked over to the empty farmyard.

Two hours later she trudged back, rosy-cheeked and smiling, carrying a winter bouquet of aesthetic weeds. Even at the age of nine, that girl believed, as James Russell Lowell put it, "A weed is no more than a flower in disguise."

My friend from the city failed to show up with his snowmobile as promised. A packed trail through the woods would have made it easier for the deer to reach later winter browsing areas.

Short daylight hours prompted us to leave by midafternoon. I don't like night driving, especially on icy roads. We had a long, cold ride home, because the car heater failed to function.

On a February morning, frost-fuzzy fingers of lacy treetops sparkled against a vibrant blue sky. Glistening white in midmorning sunlight, crystals sifted down from high branches to mingle with the snow.

Hip-deep, I waded into the fluff for a better look at a bird nest secured in the branches of a bush. Heaped full of snow, the tightly woven nest resembled a whopping ice cream cone. By now the nest's feathered architect had to be far to the south, enjoying balmy weather.

Any bird is a welcome sight in winter, and recently the Canada jay has moved into these woods. I first saw one feeding on the remains of a deer last November. Gray jays tend to stray from their natural territory during the cold months, and sometimes a big jay drops into camp looking for handouts.

The Canada jay is a handsome bird, commonly known as "camp robber." He is also called moose-bird, and Whiskey Jack—the latter a corruption of *Wis-ka-tjon,* an Indian name. Jays I've seen have not been as bold and impudent as those often described by people of the far North. In fact, up there the bird is viewed by some campers as a meat thief and a general pest.

Larger and less gaudy than his blue relative, the Canada jay has plumage of a pleasing mixture of grays, white, and black. Like the chickadee, he doesn't mind cold weather. Young jays hatch in March, even though the temperature can be well below zero. And, like a squirrel, the Canada jay tries to lay up a bountiful surplus for winter days.

While cutting firewood one day, I noticed a rabbit foot tucked low in a tree crotch. Although I didn't see him store it there, I'm quite sure it was the Canada jay that cleaned up leavings from a snowshoe hare I left on the camp table.

Abruptly the drone of a snowmobile shattered the winter serenity. The machine came growling across our cattail slough at an oblique angle. Others of its kind burst out of the woods with a roar—an invasion of sorts—snarling like mad robots unleashed from another planet.

Most of the squadron charged through snowdrifts between the beaver ponds and buzzed along the perimeter of trees before bouncing out onto the road. There they stopped in a cluster to socialize, out of earshot from me.

One straggler cut across the wild hay flat and dodged through the roadside trees. Upon seeing me, the rider pulled up and shut off the motor. Dressed in bulky snowmobile suits, everyone looks the same at a distance. This driver turned out to be a woman. It wasn't her day . . .

There I stood, momentarily irritated by this throng of noisy trespassers. I tried my best to speak calmly, politely, to the effect that I didn't allow snowmobiles in my woods. Although I had not seen the group until they reached the wide slough, my ears told me where they came from.

The woman's smile evaporated with embarrassment when I spoke, and she registered fright in a glance at the holstered pistol on my hip. I had the fleeting impression that she expected to be either arrested or shot on the spot. (In reality, I merely planned to do some target plinking later in the day.)

I accepted the woman's flustered apology for the party's intrusion, and she hurried away to join her friends. There I'm sure she quickly spread word of her encounter with the mad gunslinger. Down the road and over the hill they flew.

As the sound of their machines faded, I felt like a heel. They were probably local farmers, nice people out for a pleasant spin on a Sunday afternoon. If they had been chasing deer or harassing other wild animals, my attitude might have been justified. The event simply caught me in a circumstantial mood. Since I don't indulge in snowmobiles, perhaps I do not fully appreciate their function. I know there are plenty of people who take pleasure from that form of recreation; and there are emergencies when these snow vehicles provide the only possible mode of travel.

With too much snow in the woods for walking, Gail, Alan, and I chose to do some winter sightseeing on back roads.

The big lake a few miles away was covered with ice-fishing shanties—or was it an outhouse convention? It looked awfully bleak and cold out there on the windswept lake. This being a Sunday, smoke streamed from almost all of the tiny huts' chimneys.

On our way back to camp, as we turned off the blacktop, I gunned the motor to make it up the first hill. Our remote side road had been plowed, but the sun made parts of it slippery. The narrow winter road left barely enough room to meet another car, should one come along. Near the top of the hill, I hugged the right side, just in case. The right front wheel suddenly caught wet snow that pulled the car into banked snow up to the hood!

It all happened in a second or two. We climbed out of the left side doors to examine our predicament. There appeared to be no damage to the car, but it certainly was immobilized.

Half a mile away, cars whizzed by on the blacktop. Sister and brother set off down the hill toward the farmhouse on the highway, and I tried shoveling.

After awhile, I heard a snowmobile start up behind the farmhouse. Before long, a young man buzzed up the hill with my two grinning youngsters on the back of his machine. He said his brother was coming with a tractor. When they hooked up a heavy chain, our car yanked free.

I asked what I owed him for the trouble.

"Oh, coupla' bucks."

I thanked him profusely and paid with pleasure.

On the way back, the kids beamed: "Heck, the snowmobile ride was worth more than that!"

A mile or so down that same stretch of back road, my turn came to play good samaritan. A man had parked his pickup truck about twenty feet off the road in a clearing. His tires were made for much heavier duty than those on my car, but he was stalled on ice-filled ruts. No traction.

I opened my trunk and took over a pail of sand. A handful or two in front and back of each rear wheel did the trick. He spun out onto the road and kept going. Of course I would not have accepted payment had he offered any. I think the man was embarrassed by the ridiculously simple solution.

There are times when the ferocity of winter is overwhelming. On those frigid, blustery days, it is best to stay snug in your nest, as do the squirrels.

But to stand alone in silent woods while snow is falling—to feel the reverent hush of a winter twilight, when the white gently changes to lavender hues—to share the quiet with a fluffed-up chickadee calling softly as it flits from limb to limb . . .

These are my favorite moods of winter.

10 The Wonder of Trees

The tree which moves some to tears of joy is in the eyes of others only a green thing which stands in the way. As a man is, so he sees.
William Blake

Conifers and I have affinity; a forest isn't complete without evergreens.

One of my first endeavors on the wild 80 was to transfer an assortment of young trees to our camp clearing, because there were no evergreens close at hand. I brought in seedlings of spruce (black, white, and Norway varieties), plus tamarack and red pine. And although jack pines are not highly regarded (except by pulpwood loggers), I added a few of those too. Their aesthetic qualities fall short of other pines', but anything green is pleasing in winter. Propagation of jack pines is limited because their stubborn curved gray cones won't release seeds until a forest fire pops them open.

I remember the day I set in the first jack pine seedlings; while I leaned against the spade, a pair of amorous chipmunks raced past my feet. "It's that time of year," I smirked.

Snowshoe hares found culinary delight in my young evergreens the first winter—until I fenced in each little tree.

The smattering of pine and spruce planted around camp didn't satisfy me completely. On a misty morning in May, the boys and I picked up six hundred pine and spruce seedlings at the state nursery near Willow River. The Department of Natural Resources makes seedlings available to private land owners at a minimal cost, with the understanding that the seedlings are not dispensed for use in city yards. Tree seedlings must be ordered in quantity, well ahead of the chosen planting time.

The nursery keeps seedlings in a semirefrigerated building until sold; packed in wet moss, the young trees can be safely transported for immediate planting. We had fifty miles to go, and by sunset we had set in about two hundred pines. For overnight, we laid the remaining seedlings in shallow water (trenched them) to keep the tangled roots from drying out.

Next day, Tommy, Alan, and I finished planting the acre of pine and spruce. We put in three hundred Norway pines on the high half of a hillside slope cleared previously by bulldozer. An equal number of white spruce went to the lower half acre, bordering the slough. All seedlings were spaced six feet apart, with an access road space through the center of the patch. Since both species are native to Minnesota, I had confidence in their hardiness.

The cool, misty day made it fine for setting in trees. We often dug into submerged rocks, and in the process, one spade broke—the borrowed one, of course.

During our noon lunch break in camp, three baby gray squirrels peeked out of the duck house. Although they were not in our plans, we didn't disturb them.

When we pulled up a month later, something new had been added. A treated post with a "Tree Farm" sign had been anchored on our roadside frontage. Apparently our planting of pine and spruce had changed the classification in somebody's mind. I had never thought of the 80 as anything more than a natural woods. Somehow, I still prefer to think of it that way. "Farm" sounds too civilized, out of character.

Initially, on my exploratory hikes into the backwoods, I had to consult my compass in the tangled terrain. Once I felt eyes upon me, and in the brush crowding the old tote road a doe and her yearling studied me from behind some oaks. They waited, motionless, until I passed.

Here and there I found huge stumps, mostly pines, left by loggers in previous years of "cut and run" philosophy. And some of the pines fell victims to a fire that swept through long ago. Each black stump clung stubbornly to its position, refusing to admit defeat. Underneath the charcoal surface, the reddish stumpwood held firm against the elements.

In occasional isolated dips of terrain, a tall pine had eluded the ravages of loggers and fire. These survivors gave the woods a special charm. The stalwart trees were carrying on tradition, furnishing seeds for a new generation of pines.

I strayed farther west to a V-shaped pothole on the north boundary. Below me, native spruce punctuated the woods. In the narrow valley, I came upon one giant tree, with a trunk diameter of about two feet and a circumference of five feet, two inches. Mature hardwoods surrounding it were made to look small by comparison. Gnarled, splayed roots of the big spruce anchored it firmly to rich soil of the bottomland. A drainage brook kinked and curved a few feet away, skirting boulders and the clutching roots of trees.

I stood under the tall, straight spruce to gaze up through its rows of dark branches, thickest in the crown; about eighty-five feet tall, I estimated—almost the maximum growth for this species. Softly the wind whispered *sh-h-h* through its branches.

Most of the tree's shiny brown cones would drop off during the winter, after they opened and shed their seeds. A red squirrel had been busy shucking spruce cones to nibble on the hidden seeds. Husks lay scattered over the carpet of needles beneath the tree. No doubt the squirrel's forebears had unleashed seeds to propagate younger spruce now scattered in this sector. Whenever a seed drifted on the wind and landed in a crevice . . . melting snow or raindrops washed bits of soil over it . . . and sunlight added its touch of magic . . . the cycle went on . . .

At the base of the trunk, a blackened gash of unhealed bark testified to the tree's encounter with fire.

Bare lower branches had shed their needles long ago, but the tough gray limbs still clung tightly to the trunk. In places, teardrops of clear rosin oozed to the surface. I touched a droplet with my fingertip; it was as sticky as glue, with a pleasing aroma. In the scaly grayish-brown bark, hardened pitch filled some of the cracks. The dried rivulets were as brittle as glass. Older seepage, now turned white, reminded me of caked honey.

I reached up to strip off a few green needles for close study. The four-sided short needles were sharp, with stinger tips to prick your fingers. Could this be one of the reasons deer left spruce untouched, yet consistently munched off the long pine needles?

I broke a few spruce needles between my fingers and they gave

89

forth a pungent green smell not unpleasant to me, but lacking the fragrance of cedar or balsam fir.

Boulders four to six feet thick gave the secluded valley a strength and stability in partnership with the majestic spruce. I climbed the hill and looked back down at the towering tree. If that spruce were perched on top of a hill, it would have appeared even taller. But it might not have been as well nourished on high ground, and probably would never have attained such height. There in the valley, sheltered by hills and other trees, the venerable spruce grew to near record size. Even in dry years, its long root fingers probed fertile soil to draw in moisture and sustenance.

The exact boundary back there was a mystery to me, but I hoped the big tree was on my land. Careful study of an aerial photo would decide that. I felt covetous of the tall spruce; and yet, did it really matter whether or not I owned it? The tree held little monetary value, and even if it did, I would never cut it down. If in truth the spruce belonged to someone else, it would nevertheless be mine to admire whenever I went back that far.

I swung around to the spruce bog, which included tamaracks, white pines, and balsam fir of varying heights. On one of my preceding inspections, I had noticed some seedlings of transplantable size. The species I sought now was balsam fir, the queen of fragrance. There is nothing quite like it. No store-bought perfume compares, and I planned to take just one balsam for transplanting to my yard.

After some searching, I selected a ten-inch sprout; anything larger would be difficult to unearth and transport successfully. Even so, balsam of any size is sensitive to being moved; I would have to handle it carefully. The delicate roots were tangled in damp fibers below a surface of moss and lichens. Slowly . . . my fingers traced each root to its end . . . lightly lifting moss and all . . . until the seedling came free.

For this very purpose I had brought along a plastic bag to carry it in. First, I wrapped the roots in a handful of wet moss and decayed wood. If the roots dried before I got them into the ground back home, the little tree would never make it. The bag fit nicely into a deep pocket of my coat, with the top needles free to breathe. Every so often, a wisp of balsam fragrance drifted up to reward me.

Be it conifer or deciduous, hardwood or softwood, any kind of tree has its own special appeal, some characteristic that sets it apart. Once while exploring the backwoods, we found a distinctive old green ash in the climax stage. Its thick trunk had corklike bark, with deep fissures in a crosshatch pattern that distinguished it from neighboring trees.

When we first made a clearing for pitching our tent away from the road, I added blue beech to my list of tree types found on the wild 80. This small tree of the birch family has a tight, gray, smooth bark—much like the skin of a sturgeon. A forty-foot blue beech is a rarity; any I've found were not half that height. I left the cluster standing where I found them, in the shelter of taller trees.

On the slough edge of our campsite, a tall, umbrella-shaped elm shaded us in the heat of several summers. But soon after elms along the road became victims of Dutch elm disease, our camp elm withered away, and we made good use of the dead tree for firewood. The cross-grain of elm makes it devilish to split, even with mall and wedge; but when thoroughly dried, it supplies good heat.

I can't imagine life without trees to beautify yards and furnish shade, form windbreaks, and supply us with lumber, fuel, and paper—plus food and haven for birds and animals. And yet the benefits offered by trees are commonly taken for granted.

I'm not a mathematician, but one evening I became gripped with the notion of determining how much oxygen our woodland contributed to the atmosphere. Subtracting wetland and roads, I came up with an astounding figure: the trees on this acreage alone probably send forth *five hundred tons* of oxygen per year!

Even though I become another year older with each October, it is my favorite month. In the northern zone east of the Rockies, where trees turn color in the fall, we are treated to a glorious display of crimson and gold. Aspen, birch, maples, and tamaracks dress for their final fling of the year. By late November, the deciduous trees are bare—except for the oaks and ironwoods, so reluctant are they to part with their leaves. But the spruce and pines stay evergreen to soothe our eyes in a snowy landscape.

In any setting, the canoe birch (with its chalky white bark) is sure to catch your eye. The showy tree accents summer greenery, and even in a winter woods, the naked forms of birches cast their spell. A stand of birch is especially striking on a snow-covered hilltop, aglow in the setting sunlight against a darkening sky.

BIRCH BEAUTY

A birch tree is a winsome thing,
  So feminine, in fall or spring;
Her slender branches wave and sigh
  At carefree clouds that cross the sky.

Her trunk of basic black and white
  Is slim and graceful, styled just right,
This daintiest of forest trees
  That looks her best in fives or threes.

In party mood before the cold,
  October turns her leaves to gold;
And when the winter strips her bare,
  An empty nest bejewels her hair.
G. D.

The yellow-bellied woodpecker—often called sapsucker—will leave a ring of holes in the trunk of a birch. This bird's intemperate thirst for sap can be the downfall of a birch, but healthy trees most often heal themselves.

This brings to mind one of my pet peeves: people who cannot resist peeling the bark off birch trees. These misguided strippers take only enough "souvenir" bark to weaken the tree and shorten its life. With a break in its seal of armor, a birch is more prone to insects and disease. Decay eventually creeps in, and the tree is doomed.

I'll never understand this peculiar kind of vandalism. The guilty ones don't peel birchbark out of necessity, as the Indians did to build canoes. Most bark peelers don't even take a strip big enough to build a birdhouse. Few parks or roadside rest areas escape these strange spoilers, and when their unthinking curiosity is sated, they leave a birch with an ugly scar for succeeding travelers to behold.

A stand of aspen (a type of poplar) might be viewed by some as a "poor man's birch," but to me, the tree's bark of mottled greens is pleasing and aesthetic. Aspen is seldom used in city landscaping, so I have planted a few in my back yard.

The aspen deserves to be more popular. I see it as a happy tree. Any timorous drift of wind will stir quaking aspen leaves, setting them atwitter. They chatter softly, sharing the joy of summer sunshine. And the sweet-and-sour pungent scent of aspen enhances the forest mystique.

I give credit to aspen for the closest I have ever come to finding money growing on trees. As a boy, I rode the farm pony under popple trees to grab a handful of the shiny waxen leaves. I pretended they were dollars, and was richer then than I realized.

There is always a ready supply of dry aspen around camp. After I've been back in the snow-filled woods, nothing beats a crackling fire in the barrel stove.

Old-time loggers called the tree "quakin' asp." Now it is commonly referred to as "popple," to include its sister trees, large-tooth aspen and balm of Gilead.

This tree has always been a boon to wildlife. Beavers thrive on aspen bark; without its nourishment, they might never survive northern winters. Deer, snowshoe hares, and woodcock also rely on aspen. Wherever pulp cutters are working the woods, whitetails move in to feed on tender tips of downed tree limbs; the branches help sustain the deer until snowmelt.

Ruffed grouse would be lost without those dependable aspen buds. Clear-cut patches of aspen will support an increase in a local grouse population. These game birds need aspen in varying stages of growth—saplings for year-round cover and mature trees to provide them with a winter food supply. You, too, may have eaten aspen; it forms part of the bulk found in today's high-fiber breads.

Until recently, aspen was cut only for pulp—the very paper this is printed on probably contains aspen. Only in the last thirty-five years has this tree of the willow family come into its own, to at last gain esteem commercially. Properly dried aspen makes suitable lumber, and the soft wood takes nails readily. Using aspen in house frame construction may also relieve pressure on spruce, pine, and fir.

Aspen woodchip sheets—waferboard and chipboard—are competitive with plywood. Progress is being made toward expanding use of this most abundant tree, and before long we can expect more diversified application. In the works are cattle feed, glue, sweetener, ethanol for fuel, and increased production of fuel pellets. In areas where the trees are plentiful, aspen fuel pellets cost less than coal— and fewer pollutants are emitted in burning them.

Soon there may be other by-products developed from aspen to compete with existing petrochemicals. As technology develops, we'll no doubt see more niches for aspen to fill. Even so, there is little danger of this renewable resource being overharvested. Fast-growing aspen trees mature in about half the time needed for hardwoods.

The aspen is a prolific root spreader; as soon as a stand is cut or burned, new sprouts appear. From a few hundred existing stems, *thousands* of aspen shoots take over. In three years or less, they grow as thick as dog hair and ten feet tall. In addition, windborne seeds quickly take root on bare ground, wherever the sun reaches them.

The poplars are of ancient origin. *Populus* may refer to an early Roman expression, *arbor populi,* the people's tree.

Long ignored by loggers, this Cinderella tree has at last found the spotlight it richly deserves.

ASPEN

"They're just weed trees,"
Some people say—
But I like the way
They babble in the breeze
On a summer day.
G. D.

- GLENN DEVERY -

11 Roads

Improvement makes straight roads; but the crooked roads . . . are roads of genius.
William Blake

Finding a man with a bulldozer is a simple matter; picking one who will show up with the machine on schedule is another story.

By now I had learned to not hold my breath while waiting for any heavy-equipment operator. Every caterpillar owner I contacted left me frustrated. They were, without fail, hazy about committing themselves. Apathetic responses ranged from "Maybe . . . if the ground freezes—" to "No—too wet now" or "I would, but the rig needs fixin'. . ." And some were "tied up on another job" that never seemed to end.

In desperation, I went back to Lester, the man who first cleared a pulloff driveway for us. He was a pleasant and talkative fellow who lived on the highway a few miles away. But even Lester could not be pinned down to a date for my road clearing project.

At the rates charged by bulldozer operators, I was flabbergasted at their disinterest. My credit rating wasn't *that* bad—I always paid off when an assignment was completed.

Nothing improved their ways as the hourly rate climbed over the years—$15 per hour, then $25, up to $35, $50, and $70 per hour after the price of diesel fuel skyrocketed.

Most people in the hinterlands will have nothing to do with life in the fast lane. Their attitude is probably due more to independence than to laziness. Some of the "natives" run small farms, or hold down a job in town to improve their standard of living.

But you will find some bona fide loafers out there, just as you will in the city. One such bulldozer man gave me fits. Whenever I drove up to his house, he was "gone to town." His wife and kids were always home, and so was his big machine. I think beer became his career. Twice I bumped into him away from home. The first time, his 'dozer needed fixing, then he'd wrap up the job "in no time." On the second occasion, he actually came to look at my woods, and spent half the time bragging about his talent for poaching deer. After that, I lost interest in him.

On a Monday morning in February, the phone rang just as I took hold of the doorknob to leave home for the 80. Jake was calling from Larsville to tell me he couldn't keep today's appointment for bulldozing. (So what else is new?) "See you tomorrow instead," he promised.

With the car already loaded, I drove up a day early to take care of odds and ends. I passed my tree-farm sign at the roadside, and continued to Lindstroms' driveway. If Jake decided to bring the bulldozer in on high ground tomorrow, this would be the place to enter.

It took me a while to hacksaw off their small padlock, as prearranged with the owners. I replaced it with a heavier new brass model. One of the keys would go to the Lindstroms, and I'd keep the spare for emergencies.

A foot of snow covered the ground, and yet I saw no animal tracks around camp, not a snowshoe, grouse, weasel, or even a field mouse. Winter brings hard times to wildlife, and by February it takes a toll.

I struck out for the woods on a packed snowmobile track left by the firewood cutter. It made for much easier walking while it lasted.

By dusk I came back from the woods with a ravenous appetite. Two plump cheeseburgers, sourdough bread, and fried parsnips took care of that—topped off with apple pie and coffee. I stoked up the fire and turned in for the night. Tomorrow could be a big day.

I woke up cold at dawn. A fire soon took the bite out of the air, and fifteen minutes later I could no longer see my breath inside the shack.

Nine o'clock came, and no bulldozer.

Some of the pine seedlings around camp had to be marked with red plastic ribbon to guide the bulldozer man against overrunning them—that is, when, or if, he showed up.

Late in the afternoon, I heard rumbling down the road; a big truck came over the hill with the bulldozer on a flatbed, followed by a pickup truck. While he unchained the big machine, Jake explained the delay.

"Been losing compression on my truck," he said. "My wife followed in the pickup in case it quit on me. I'll clear off the snow here for a turnaround, then go home and see if I can fix it tonight. Be back in the morning . . . if I can—"

He rolled the caterpillar off the flatbed, plowed snow down to frozen ground, parked the machine, and left. I certainly hoped the bulldozer wasn't suffering from any ailments similar to his truck's. We needed a better access road, and delays were straining my patience.

In a way, it's a good thing I was alone on this trip. Whenever I suggested cutting a new stretch of road through our woods, my youngest son winced in apprehension. Some things are sacred. If left to him, road building on the wild 80 would be forbidden. "But Dad," he implored, "if you get *too* many roads, it won't be *natural!*"

I understood his viewpoint: the wild and free state of woodland has unique appeal. Daniel Boone or John Muir would have agreed with him.

Over the years, I have proceeded cautiously in expanding woods roads, trying to justify each new segment. In the first stage, we simply bulldozed brush and fallen trees from the existing logging trail. That made hiking easier, and the winding east-to-west pathway gave us security. A mile of timbered hills and brush-rimmed potholes was enough to disorient us as newcomers.

Before the brushy tote road was cleared, we sometimes strayed off it while exploring. And not surprisingly, we often found ourselves "temporarily misplaced"—like the bedraggled mountain man who finally reappeared after being lost in the wilderness for two weeks. Asked if he'd been lost, the grizzled woodsman replied, "Nope . . . wa'nt lost . . . jest a mite confused fer a few days."

I recall one early hike with two of the boys and their sister. The deep woods didn't frighten Gail; she rather enjoyed moseying off by herself. On this day, the boys and I elected to continue into the back 80. The resourceful eight-year-old announced that she would follow the trail back to the hilltop overlooking the slough, and meet us there later. I hesitated. No, she assured me, she would *not* get lost. Don't worry.

As we rounded a bend in the logging road, I looked back, and Gail was completely absorbed in watching a butterfly.

Two or three hours later the boys and I came back by the place; no Gail in sight. Calling her name brought no response. "Prob'ly back in camp," her brothers offered nonchalantly. *They* never worry. We proceeded to the hilltop where she had promised to wait for us. When I called out, there was no answer. I began to berate myself for allowing the little girl to stray off on her own. I kept yelling "Gail!" as we picked our way through the brushy hillside.

Near the slough edge at the bottom of the hill, a squeaky voice at last reached my ears. Relieved, I hurried down there. She was fine, not scared, and furthermore she insisted that she was *not lost.* Maybe a ways off the trail, she admitted.

At the time, she wasn't crying, but I thought I detected signs that she had been. I led her out of the weeds and brush toward familiar ground. To this day, Gail maintains that, given time, she would have found her way back to camp, thank you.

As the seasons rolled by, I dreamed of improved road access to the back woods. Why did we need more roads, anyway? There wouldn't be any caravan of covered wagons rolling westward looking for the promised land. In fact, would not a better road be an invitation to trespassers? That could spell added danger of fire in the woods from tobacco smokers and from campfires left unattended.

Also, uninvited hikers might include the scourge of litter louts, and there surely is nothing aesthetic about discarded beverage cans and bottles amongst wildflowers.

Road access to a private woods invites other serious problems, such as poachers and timber thieves. If the trail will support a pickup truck or four-wheel-drive vehicle, game hogs are liable to take advantage of it, in or out of the established hunting seasons.

As soon as the new road is completed, no matter how rough it might be, there is a necessity for more than "Keep Out" signs. A gate is the next step, or at least a heavy steel cable padlocked around pillars or sizable trees on both sides of the entrance.

In remote areas, theft of firewood or sawlogs is more difficult to avoid. Unless you live on the property, or have a faithful neighbor to keep vigil, wood robbers can make a profitable haul in just a few hours.

In recent years, black walnut has become the most valuable hardwood in the United States, if not in the world. A top-grade mature walnut tree may be worth thousands of dollars. With proper equipment, thieves can creep in on a stormy night to steal a previously chosen tree. In an hour or so, two or three men can fell the most valuable specimen, chain-saw it into logs, and load up, and be a hundred miles away by morning.

The few walnut trees I have planted on the wild 80 are near the road, but they will be safe for half a century; it can take up to seventy-five years for this slow-growing hardwood to reach marketable size.

Of course, a rough road through your woods offers advantages, too. On the plus side, access is a must in case of a forest fire. And how else can you reach choice sawtimber or stands of popple for pulpwood cutting? The most simple methods of forest management require ingress-egress. After the bulldozer crashes through, downed hardwoods can be salvaged for firewood.

I won't soon forget the fall when I dragged a buck through the woods, with no snow on the ground. After huffing and puffing up hills and down for more than a mile, you can bet that I fervently wished for a functional road over every blessed yard of that haul.

The deer quickly make use of new roads. During November, when the rutting season is in full swing, bucks leave "scrapes" in the middle of woods trails. A buck checks these every day or so (mostly at night) to see if any romantically inclined doe has entered his bailiwick.

All deer favor the edges of a freshly cut road, where handy branch tips offer them an easy meal. And as time passes, those road borders (now exposed to more sunlight) will send up luscious new sprouts for the whitetails to feed on.

Wednesday morning came on cold, about fifteen degrees below zero. That didn't matter, because at 8:30 Jake showed up. I poured a cup of coffee for him in the warm shack, only half joking about it costing me fifty dollars an hour for coffee breaks.

After I had waited so long, it did my heart good to see the bulldozer in action, scraping off a clearing toward the shack. We had spent long, laborious hours in hacking and grubbing out stumps here by hand. In half an hour the 'dozer removed brush and small trees, stumps, boulders, and frozen topsoil to widen the clearing. Although further leveling would be necessary after the ground thawed, now I could drive the car in behind the shack. With the snow shoved aside, it felt wonderful to walk on solid earth again.

Back when the ponds were dug, the dragline had left a huge mound of dirt between the camp clearing and the middle pond. It came in handy now for road fill. Protected by a solid crust of frost nearly two feet deep, the pile of snow-capped clay bristled with willow shoots. It looked impregnable, but the big blade probed the rock-hard mound until it found a weak spot for a start. Gradually, larger chunks broke free under persistent prodding from the heavy machine.

I stood on top of a ten-foot pile of snow and debris to watch the bulldozer. Each lumpy mass of dirt added height to the road between ponds. Caterpillar treads packed it down. Near pond's edge, it scraped into soft clay, and water oozed up. At one point I thought the rig might get bogged down.

When the mound was half removed, Jake pointed in front of the 'dozer. I couldn't hear him over the grinding machine, so I jumped off the pile to have a look. A groggy woodchuck, rousted unceremoniously from his winter snooze, crept away in slow motion. Being a true hibernator, he would have a barely perceptible pulse rate at this time of year. I could do nothing but guide the staggering woodchuck toward a snow covered brushpile; his chances of surviving now were nil—the cold, a mink, or a coyote would surely get him.

Removal of the earth mound left us without an observation point to view the ponds; but come spring, we'd be able to see the water from our improved clearing. And the raised roadbed between the two upper ponds shored up the beaver dam.

At long last we could move those two concrete culverts from along our entrance off the gravel road. They had been plunked down seven years earlier, awaiting placement. Jake got behind the first one with his 'dozer blade and rolled it along the dirt road to the north end of the island. He would position it later, below the beaver dam over there.

We took a lunch break in the comfort of the shack, and Jake told me his flatbed story. He bought the heavy-duty trailer from a man down in the Twin Cities, but when he went to get it, the rig was gone. One of the previous owner's drivers stole it and drove to Texas. Police had located it, but they couldn't return it to Minnesota. Jake had to drive to Texas and bring it home.

In the afternoon, his itinerant "C-7" cleared about four hundred yards of trees between our boundary and Lindstrom's driveway. This was all high ground, and would make a good emergency entrance during wet weather—or in case of a forest fire. Together we selected a route, avoiding the larger oaks.

The growling bulldozer leaned heavily into each big tree's trunk until it tilted. When the machine's stubborn force snapped off the tree's frozen roots, the tree cracked and crashed with a muffled "whoof" into deep snow. Black dirt, clay, and rocks were then exposed below frostline for easy grading.

When the short winter day ended, Jake parked the 'dozer in our camp clearing, and drove the flatbed home.

After being out in the cold all day, I welcomed stove heat. A big meal put me to sleep early.

On Thursday morning, before tackling the little hill on our boundary, I wanted the ridge road snowplowed down to the nine cords of firewood at the south border.

That done, Jake came back to the little hill and shut off the motor to eat his lunch. We studied the neck of the slough to be filled in with the hill's contents. I returned to the shack for a bite to eat, and he began pushing over trees, prior to disemboweling the hill.

A half hour later I glanced out the window toward the island, and here he came with the bulldozer! Something wrong; he pulled into the clearing and climbed down from the cab.

"Broke a part on the arm behind the blade," he lamented. "Hafta' haul it into town to get the damned thing welded."

He rolled the machine onto his flatbed, secured it, and thundered off down the road. A disappointing delay, for both of us; but "those are the breaks," you might say.

While waiting for Jake to return from town with the repaired bulldozer, I went back out to examine the little hill across from the island. Before the sun dropped, I snapped a picture; in less than twenty-four hours the hill would no longer be there.

The elevation offered a good view of the quarter mile of beaver-flooded slough to the south. On warm weather trips into the back-woods, I often paused there to watch the ducks. Mallards liked to laze in the sun on floating hummocks, feeding at leisure on green glop in the shallows.

Now in winter garb, the long strip of backwater lay frozen solid. Brown, forlorn weeds stood anchored to their chins in ice and snow. Down at the far end, I could see the snow-covered hump of the beavers' latest lodge.

Deer enjoyed browsing on the brushy island below, but after it became waterlogged, they only used it during the cold months. There they could feed on moose willow and red osier dogwood, or bed down in the sun, sheltered from cold winds by the uphill timber.

I walked across the top of the little hill, and had mixed feelings about scalping it. The thought of changing the ancient terrain bothered me a bit—and yet we needed the dirt and rocks to fill in the narrow strip of slough to connect with the island's north end. The hill sat in perfect proximity for this purpose. A few boulders protruded from its surface, and it might even be hiding a gravel deposit. In case it consisted only of rocks and clay, it would still be excellent for building up a road crossing.

As I studied the self-sufficient little hill, it took on a personality of its own. Overlooking the island and slough, it was surrounded on three sides by higher slopes. The snow hid drainage gullies that curved around its base.

Oak trees in mixed sizes covered most of the hill, with a few scattered birches in contrast. I inspected depressions in the deep snow where deer had pawed down to hard ground to search for acorns, much the way elk paw for buried grasses. For some reason, deer favored this particular hill over others nearby. Hereafter, the white-tails would have to choose other oaks.

A bountiful crop of acorns each year is crucial to forest creatures.

The very survival of certain animals may depend on these nourishing nuts. Deer, bear, grouse, wood ducks, jays, and crows—even bugs and people eat acorns. Squirrels and chipmunks would be lost without them. With smaller animals, there is much stealing of each other's hordes, even when pickings are good. The theory of wildlife seems to be "You can never get too many acorns."

Population levels of animals and birds can fluctuate in direct correlation to the year's supply of acorns. In nature's food chain, even predators are affected by a short crop of these nutritious nuts; scarcity of acorns means fewer animals or birds for them to choose from.

The tallest oak grew in the center of the independent hill. Somebody's weathered deer stand perched high off the ground on a sturdy limb.

I recalled watching a pair of chipmunks gamboling about the tree's base; they had been storing food in holes under the roots. And one summer a lone blackberry bush cropped up a few feet away. I had hopes of it turning into a private berry patch; unfortunately, it lasted for just one season. No doubt a snowshoe found it quite delectable in frigid February.

The little hill probably hadn't changed shape much in ten thousand years, since the glaciers melted and tumbled it into this form. Only the surface trees and vegetation had come and gone over the centuries, while the boulders rested below.

Before the 'dozer broke down from striking a huge boulder buried in the ground, it had pushed over a few oak trees on top of the hill. The prostrate trunks were nearly submerged in snow. Each fallen tree's mass of frozen roots and topsoil revealed signs of gravel and clay. Tomorrow the growling machine would return to bare the hill's contents, and the slumbering boulders would see daylight for the first time in a hundred centuries.

But I wouldn't be there to watch. After three days and nights in the woods, I had commitments back in the city.

*   *   *

Two weeks later I drove into the camp clearing, slammed the car

105

door, and hurried over to the island. Fresh snow covered the ground, disguising evidence of the bulldozer's earth-wrenching activity. The little hill was gone. I took an "after" picture to compare with the previous snapshot.

When I kicked snow aside, it revealed a mixture of stones, gravel, and clay. The neck of the slough had been solidly bridged, with one concrete culvert seated in and ready for spring flowage. The conglomeration of rocks and gravelly soil tapered to a depth of six feet across the drainage trough. No more would we have to use the narrow beaver dam (like walking a tightrope) to avoid getting wet feet.

Although I missed the little hill, in its place the bulldozer left a nice level clearing. Rocks of all sizes lined the edges, including some boulders three feet in diameter. To my relief, the long view of the beaver water backup had not been jeopardized, because the hill had only been bladed down to half its original height.

One thing I hadn't noticed before: the rock-filled road sloping down from the new gravel plateau pointed straight to the shack a quarter of a mile away. I liked the view, and after a long hike in the far woods, pausing there gave me a feeling of being close to home. The island road followed a sweeping curve of the beaver dam toward our camp.

The remodeled terrain turned out better than I expected—almost like having your cake and eating it too. The firewood cutter had already stacked about two cords of oak, salvaged from the little hill. And wherever he left fallen trees, hungry deer moved in to feed on the tips of branches.

All in all, I considered it a fair trade-off.

12 March Odyssey

Daffodils,
That come before the swallow dares, and take
The winds of March with beauty.
William Shakespeare

Winter began to wear thin by the middle of March, and a softer wind came in from the south. The last mile of gravel road had thawed down about four inches, and my car chugged along in a pair of muddy ruts. I was glad no other vehicle met me on the narrow road, forcing me to risk pulling onto the soggy shoulder.

An impassable snowbank blocked the driveway entrance. I parked on the road and tromped a trail into camp. The flat-roofed shack supported a thick layer of snow, like too much frosting on a cake.

Tracks of a bobcat crossed the camp clearing and snowshoe hares were prevalent, but the wildcat hadn't captured anything in the vicinity.

Inside the shack, surprised at my intrusion, a little red squirrel scrambled about. He dashed into a hole in the box spring to hide, then panicked and ran outside through a secret exit.

Dry kindling produced a quick fire in the barrel stove. While the shack warmed up, I nailed a bluebird house to the "Tree Farm" post, faced away from the road. The birdhouse would be handy for periodic inspection.

A rooster pheasant crowed from a hayfield down the road; the stylish import was expanding his range. On this quiet morning, I could hear the flap of the rooster's wings. Untended farm fields nearby offered plenty of weedy cover, and pheasants do thrive on weed seeds. But coyotes, owls, and other predators would be waiting to put a strain on the newcomer's existence.

I took the aluminum ladder over to inspect the wood-duck house;

it needed cleaning before the woodies returned to raise their broods.

There were animal teeth and claw marks around the entrance hole, and I lifted the lid to peer into the nest. To my surprise, there was a duck egg sticking out of the feathery residue. I took off a glove and lifted it out. Strange that the egg did not crack during the winter. When I grabbed a handful of feathers, a few bones came with them. Duck bones. A mink or a weasel must have killed the mother duck on the nest, and devoured her. As for the possibility of an owl being the villain, only a screech owl would be small enough to enter the four-inch hole.

By the time I had cleaned out the old nest, I had six spoiled duck eggs in a pan. It struck me as peculiar that the eggs had not been eaten too.

From there I carried the ladder out to the island to straighten a rusty ten-gallon milk can we'd hung on a dead elm. I wasn't sure the ducks would make use of it, but the can was the proper size, with an entrance hole.

Drowned, bedraggled trees stood in ice above the beaver dam. After spring thaw, I wouldn't be able to get out there.

A grouse exploded from a patch of weeds on the island. One at a time, three more burst out of brush fringes, and a fifth bird stepped nervously away through the underbrush. This may have been one of their mating areas.

Hammer in hand, I climbed the ladder and clanked off the battered milk can lid to peek inside. It was filled almost to the top with downy cattail fur. When I reached in to grab a handful, something squirmed out of my gloved fingers. Certainly not a duckling this early in the year? Before I had time for another guess, a big-eyed mouse came out and crept across the top of the tilted can. She paused in the sun, dark eyes glistening, about a foot in front of my face. I've never had a better chance to study a live mouse up close. The smooth gray fur on her back and the silky white underside were immaculately groomed. Her dainty pink feet spread out on the rusted metal surface, and she didn't quite know what to do next.

For a fleeting moment, I tried to set the hammer down to pull a camera from my pocket, but the movement sent her scurrying down the tree trunk. When I tapped the milk can again, another mouse came out and followed the first. Then another, and still a fourth mouse headed down to hide in weeds and snow.

Before this, I hadn't thought of mice as tree climbers. I cleaned out the makeshift duck house and hung the can back on the tree.

At the edge of the gravel plateau, I chose a solitary tree for another bluebird house. Although bluebirds prefer open fields and meadows, this was the best I could offer. At least the ground-feeding "blue robins," as the pilgrims called them, could look out on the clearing and part of the new woods road. It might suit them, if a pair of these scarce birds ever found the dwelling.

Ordinarily, March is a very windy month in Minnesota, but today there was no wind. When I turned to investigate a faint rustling in dry leaves, a sprightly chipmunk scrambled in and out of a deadfall— proof that his kind survived alteration of the little hill. When at last he came close enough, I snapped his picture before he skittered away.

Along the ridgetop, a porcupine had stripped four or five maples during the winter. I had seen one sunning himself on a limb over there in the fall. Now he was probably napping under one of the brushpiles left by the firewood cutter.

Hunger pangs sent me to camp for a snack. On the way, I examined two hollow sections of an ash tree that I planned to turn into duck nesting shelters.

At the shack, with both daylight and my energy limited, I decided to repair the front door. Tomorrow, when I'd have more time and renewed strength, I'd finish the duck houses. Even *hollow* ash logs are heavy to carry up a ladder.

In late afternoon, the owls hooted their positions to each other far back in the woods. Soft wind currents rustled dry marsh grasses bordering the frozen ponds. This was a quiet time between seasons, when the marsh waited for spring thaw and return of the waterfowl. The woods were hushed before the birds arrived, and I thought of Rachel Carson's *Silent Spring*.

Toward evening, a subdued warbling came from the point of trees across the wild hay meadow. After some scanning, I managed to pick out the silhouette of an early bird of unknown species. He was perched near the top of the tallest tree over there, softly, shyly singing—testing his melody in private. He only sang for a little

111

while, and then gave up. There were no other birds around to hear him. In a few more weeks he should have a better audience.

At sundown, the gentle wind subsided. A crackling flurry caused me to look over at the point near the round pond, where a pair of grouse had settled in the treetops. They were stretching their necks to pick at buds for an evening meal. At dusk, one bird abruptly peeled off in a speedy glide to the pond willows; the other stayed put for the night.

Daylight faded fast after sunset. A crescent sliver of pale gold accented the purple sky. It soon became the only source of light, a celestial ornament pinned onto a vast expanse of dark velvet. An hour later, the blurred outline of the moon's circle became visible before it retired behind the black horizon to the southwest. Countless stars came out to enliven the heavens.

By this time I had forsaken the outdated kerosene lantern for a new gas model that cast more light; but the penalty was its constant hissing noise. On this occasion the campstove balked, as if jealous of the gas-gulping rival. Deep snow made it difficult to cook over a campfire, so I ended up preparing a slow supper on the barrel stove.

Logs popped while I sat on the bunk bed scrawling notes of the day's events by lantern light. Fresh air, outdoor exercise, heat from the stove . . . all combined to make me drowsy. I banked up the fire and turned in early. Melting snow dripped off the roof to lull me to sleep.

Before dawn, the yap of a coyote broke the silence. Short choppy notes. Had he found his quarry, or was he only trying to locate other members of the pack?

In the morning, just enough red coals lingered in the ashes for rekindling the fire. While I waited for the teakettle to boil, I stepped outside to greet a warm, windless, foggy morning. Moisture-laden air smelled of spring.

I followed the snow-carved path out to the road to absorb the eerie hush. In the fog's confining half-light, nearby trees took on the aspect of a soft pencil sketch on off-white paper. For the time being, fog erased the surrounding woods. There was no sound. My world had shrunk to a hazy circle that could be measured only in yards or meters. I listened to the awesome silence, and peered toward the invisible farm buildings that I knew were over there.

After breakfast, the morning sun began to conquer the fog. From roadside I could make out the ghostly forms of the farmhouse and barn.

I went over to breathe in the awakening smells of spring beside the ponds, and broad wings waved a pair of great blue herons over the slough from the south. Early arrivals. As a rule, herons are loners, but mating time was fast approaching. The majestic couple drifted over me, just thirty feet above my head. Their powerful wing strokes made flight look deceptively simple; spotlighted by the rising sunrays, the huge birds took graceful command of the sky. With necks coiled back and chests puffed out, the herons' body attitude suggested smugness at the striking picture they presented.

March can present a varied bag of tricks, ranging from fog to blizzard; this time it offered its good side. I walked down the road and plunged through deep snow to check on the apple trees. All three were fenced, but because of the snow depth, hungry hares might nip off the branches. The bunnies were on an "up cycle"; their tracks and trails were everywhere. As a precaution, I packed down a circle around the fencing of each apple tree.

Today's goal was to hang those two hollow log sections as duck houses beside the beaver ponds. In camp, I sawed pieces of scrap boards for tops and bottoms to seal off each natural cavity.

Back on the island, the tip of my chain saw bored a square hole into both hollow chunks of log. Although it strains a saw to use it that way, I had no alternative. After nailing on the bottom and lid boards, I positioned a vertical 2 x 4 on each log's backside for spiking to a tree.

It soon became evident that this should be a two-man job. Without four arms, I simply could not safely carry one of those heavy ash "houses" up the ladder by myself. To accomplish that, I'd need a block and tackle, which I didn't have along. Risking a fall while alone in the woods was nothing short of foolhardy.

Wood ducks, and possibly goldeneyes, should be arriving any day, and by the time I could return with a partner, they surely would have moved on to find a home elsewhere. There had to be an alternative.

Individual cords of wood stacked between trees offered me the solution. The woodpiles were about four feet high. I climbed up, and with an added log for a prop, successfully hoisted one duck house into position. Before it could slip off, I spiked it onto the tree trunk, facing water to the east. This left the entrance hole eight or nine feet above ground level—not the fifteen feet recommended by Ducks Unlimited, but for now it would have to do. With help later, I could move the shelters if the tree-nesting ducks shunned them.

I repeated this maneuver with the other house about thirty yards away. A few saplings had to be cleared by hatchet to allow free flight access.

From the gravel plateau, my view of the quarter mile of beaver backup was blocked by a grandaddy of a popple. It stood at water's edge, and must have been two feet thick at the base. For some time I had wanted that doomed tree out of my line of vision.

During the previous autumn, a beaver had gnawed around the trunk and given up. Once a beaver starts on a tree, and then quits for reasons of his own, he seldom if ever returns to finish the job. Tree size or toughness is not the reason he abandons it; I've found sizable oaks chewed off at the base. Maybe this chomper didn't like the taste or smell, or something scared him off.

To reach the big aspen, I had to climb over a tangled mass of dead trees toppled by the bulldozer when it leveled the little hill. In the process, dry branches snapped, and I startled three tiny birds, common redpolls. They flitted out from the downhill side, and paused a moment to study this noisy intruder. Thoreau called them "delicate, crimson-tinged birds." This trio wouldn't stay in my woods long. The pretty, fluffy little "snowbirds" were a long way from their summer home in the far North, where redpolls favor arctic nesting grounds.

My chain saw tore through the trunk, and the heavy tree crashed onto ice of the slough. A cloud of cattail cotton floated on the air. The old popple would soon decay in tepid water during the summer. Its fibers were destined to join the buildup of humus from previous layers of marsh plants. Temporarily, the prostrate tree might serve as a summer bridge for raccoons in search of frogs.

With the day's major exercise over, I paused to rest on a cord of oak at the edge of the gravel plateau. Before long, melting snow would fill the marsh and overflow the ponds below. In the distance, woodsmoke curled out of the shack chimney, a picture of serenity.

13 Almost Spring

Teaching barren moors to smile,
painting pictures mile on mile . . .
Ralph Waldo Emerson

I like to wander through the woods in April. It is easier then to peruse terrain, before plush greenery fills in the open spaces. As a rule, snow is gone, except for a few die-hard patches in sheltered nooks. The earliest wildflowers are asserting themselves, and trees are cautiously frizzing out with leaves. Insects have not yet gained a foothold, and the air is sweet with the promise of spring.

From beneath a brushpile at the edge of camp, I scooped up enough snow to cool my perishables. The dog charged over to see what delicacy I had found there.

A deer bounded across the farm hayfield, and flocks of geese sailed high to the north. Ducks were coming back from the South, cruising the ponds for nesting sites.

On the raised road between ponds, a few thick chunks of frozen clay defied the sun. Beavers left wide footprints in mud along the dam, and a steady flow of brownish water poured from underneath the muddy, settling road into the second pond. If ever I was to succeed in salvaging the sunken culvert, this is where it should go.

At the north end of the island, beavers had stuffed the concrete culvert full of sticks and tangled mats of marsh roots. I reached into the cold water to pull out debris and speed up flowage. Fast water soon cleared itself over the bed of multicolored stones below the culvert.

Wooded hillsides were coming alive with drainage brooklets, and the sound of trickling water mingled with birdsong. On my way inland, I handcast white clover seed along the new woods road.

Up on the gravel plateau, a few obnoxious weeds were already poking through the gritty soil. On a bend in the woods road, the track of a bear cub marked a mudhole. Someday I might get a glimpse of him.

Beyond the plateau, a huge dead oak had at last hit the ground. The sturdy old tree had held vigil above the former little hill for perhaps a hundred years. Dry bark had cracked and fallen off its trunk long before the oak finally collapsed.

Dying trees pick their own point of landing, most often across the trail; but this one dropped conveniently uphill beside the woods road. I surmised that the squirrels and woodpeckers would miss this familiar hollow oak with its roomy shelter holes.

Nearby, I picked up an elongated, roughly serrated shell that showed teethmarks—a butternut! There must be a tree somewhere in the vicinity, if only I could find it.

Hungry deer had nipped the tops off most of our three hundred laboriously planted pine seedlings. To save the few remaining pines, we had tried a makeshift scarecrow of old clothes to discourage browsing deer, but it did not stop them.

When I came over a rise in the trail, a downy woodpecker hid behind the trunk of a rotting aspen until I passed by. Judging by the pecked hole up there on my side of the tree, she intended to keep her nesting place a secret.

There is a common saying in this state: "If you don't like Minnesota's weather, just wait a few hours and it will change." By the following morning, four inches of new snow blanketed the woods. Even this late in April, winter was not ready to surrender. During the night, the northeast side of tree trunks had been plastered with white. Low, snow-laden branches touched the ground, and bushes drooped with their burden.

By midmorning, the sun began to do its duty. At first the topmost branches of a tall maple shifted in the rising breeze. A few clumps of wet snow slid off and dropped to the ground, and the limbs regained their normal composure. Soft, muffled plops gained momentum as other trees followed suit.

I put on my boots for a stroll along the woods path. Snow-smothered branches closed off part of the walkway, forcing me to stoop under loaded bushes and low limbs. After a gob of snow landed on the back of my neck, I turned up my coat collar for protection.

Tracks of a mink crossed the path, leaving a shallow furrow in the melting snow. On my way to the ponds, I stepped off the trail to follow grouse tracks, and a cottontail bounded out of some brush. He'd been soaking up morning sunlight beside a log.

As I watched globs of snow plummeting from treetops, an abnormal shape caught my eye. Up ahead, some kind of big bird sat perched on a low limb. An owl would not perch that close to the ground. I used the continuous plop-plop of snow slipping off the trees to disguise my footsteps. Slowly, I crept closer—fifty feet . . . forty feet . . . thirty-five . . . I peeked out from behind a tree, and the bird hadn't spooked. It was a black-crowned night heron in silhouette against the pond. As quietly as possible, I took out my camera and focused for distance. The heron was dozing in the sun, with his bill buried in puffy chest feathers. I picked an opening through snow-laden bushes and waited, camera at the ready. At last the heron pulled out his bill and partially unkinked his neck. The peculiar plume of extended feathers curved five or six inches over his back. Now or never. *Click!* With that the bird unlimbered and flapped silently off across the slough.

Around a curve in the shoreline, I heard something thrashing in the water and tangled weeds. When I eased over to satisfy my curiosity, there was nothing in sight. I waited. Suddenly it started again. A few yards away, I caught the flash of dark brown—a mink. He was probably in hot pursuit of a frog or a muskrat, and I had only a quick look at his tail and hindquarters in the weeds at waterline. Camera in hand, I hoped to be ready when he came up on shore to devour the kill. But the mink must have missed his target, because he never appeared again.

On the sunny side of the point, I inspected my fenced-in tamarack. It now stood four feet tall. Barring the hazards of weather, sharp teeth, and sawflies, it might someday reach a height of seventy feet. I stroked one of the budding branch tips. Ever so soft light-green needles were emerging in tight brushlike clusters.

Pussy willows bloomed at ponds' edge to put a whiff of spring in the air. Their soft, furry buds have universal appeal, and black

119

willow branches have a pleasant, lingering fragrance.

Some years ago, and quite by chance, I discovered that it makes no sense to place pussy willows in water. It only hastens growth of the buds; they soon swell up and then drop off. A tall, dry vase is best. The silken tufts will hold their form and cling to the stems until next year's crop is ready—if you want to keep them that long.

The same is true for cattails. I never put them into water. Instead, I fill a wide-mouth ceramic pot with six inches of dry sand, and jam the cut stems into the sand to hold them in a firm arrangement. With this dry treatment, the brown felt tubes won't pop open and fill the room with cattail cotton. I always cut cattails in August, before they get too fat. The slim ones last longer.

During the night the weather turned cold and windy. It wasn't easy to leave my warm sleeping bag, but I crawled out and went for a morning stroll.

Crows were clamoring out on the point, probably harassing an owl. I started down the trail to investigate.

New ice covered most of the ponds, but a pair of mallards were taking advantage of a fringe of open water embracing the shoreline. Sheltered from the wind, they were tipping and bobbing for precious green sprouts.

When I came into view, the ducks sat suspended on the water like magnificently painted wooden decoys. The drake wore his finest mating plumage, with a tight spit-curl tail and his head a deep velvet green. Both ducks eyed me with suspicion. I stood perfectly still, waiting for their sudden straight-up rise and call of alarm. In their fashion, waterfowl have to make life-or-death decisions. But this time the ducks swam warily away through last year's tattered cattails. In a few weeks I might see the hen mallard leading a string of fuzzy ducklings across the ponds.

The raw northeast wind drove a steady torrent of snow pellets in a nearly horizontal flow, and the point of trees took on a milky haze. To shield my face from the icy barrage, I pulled up my coat collar and moved toward the noisy crows. Their frenzied calling centered on a Norway pine. Walking in slow motion, I tried to see how close I could get to them. Most of the crows promptly went quiet and scattered in all directions. It is next to impossible to catch crows by surprise.

I eased up closer for a better look, and spotted a dark ball of feathers on a limb some twenty feet high. A great horned owl faced the ice-laden wind. As he perched with his back toward me, only his tail and wingtips moved with the frigid air currents. Apparently he had not heard or seen my approach against the wind. I tried for a better view, keeping him in sight, and managed to get within ten yards of his tree.

Now I could see one eye glaring down at me through the top of his ruffled head feathers. The so-called "horns" of *Bubo virginianus* took shape against the gray sky. So . . . he knew I was there all the time! And yet the owl chose to stay put. Neither crows nor man could scare him into moving this blustery day.

I wondered if he might have a mate nesting nearby. In better weather, I'd scan those trees again.

For awhile I stood behind a big elm to escape the biting wind. Just as the owl turned his head to put me in full focus of his glare, a crow came by and "caw-caw-cawed" at him. Other crows answered in the distance, and almost immediately they were there in force to join in the fracas.

How many centuries, I pondered, have crows and owls been mortal enemies? The crows, of course, can only make pests of themselves when they discover an owl in their territory. Lacking the killing talons of owls, crows must rely on their superior brain power. In daylight, crows are too active and wary to fear an owl, but instinct tells them that owls kill their roosting brethren at night. Crows, in turn, are not exactly harmless. They sometimes rob other birds' nests to eat the eggs—and occasionally the fledglings.

I watched the timeless conflict until the crows gave up and left again. The cold wind pushed me back toward the path. A few steps away a chipmunk skittered across matted leaves beneath bare trees hugging the shoreline. He was the first of his kind I had seen this year, and he could not have been out of hibernation for long. Chippies always look so—well, "chipper" in their bright-eyed pursuits. With quick bursts of speed, the chipmunk's legs disappeared in a blur until he stopped to arch up and study me. This perky little woods scamp had better maintain his habit of traveling only by day, or the great owl out there . . .

Before I walked another twenty paces, I came upon scattered feathers. A ruffed grouse had met its doom here, but I could not prove the owl guilty; circumstantially, perhaps—although a hawk, weasel, or fox might have been the culprit.

When grouse cycles are down, some bird hunters tend to blame hawks and owls. Most of an owl's diet, however, comes from mice and other nocturnal rodents. The owl hunts only live prey, and generally his victim is light enough to carry off. But those lethal, curved talons are capable of taking larger prey—rabbits and hares, for instance. And skunks are not immune to airborne attackers. That power-packed scent will not deter a great horned owl. Nor is a porcupine safe; the barbed quills cannot penetrate an owl's feathers. Even small dogs and prowling housecats can fall victim to a great horned owl, heaviest of the species.

This owl may sport a five-foot wingspan. And his feathers are marvelously designed to muffle all sound in flight. An experiment once tested an owl's sight and hearing to prove his ability. A mouse and an owl were placed in a closed room. The total darkness didn't handicap the owl. With unerring accuracy, he swooped down to pin the mouse.

The binocular vision of owls is far superior to humans', especially in poor light. Owls require only one tenth—possibly as little as one hundredth—of the light we need to pick out an object.

If you can see an owl's head move when he snaps it around, you certainly don't need glasses. He swings his head to take in 180 degrees from either side. It only *looks* as though his head goes all the way around, it happens so fast.

An owl's ears consist of holes covered with flaps in the eye ring. One is set higher than the other to help him pinpoint sound. (In comparison, we need two eyes in order to judge distance.)

As for the "horns" of the big owl, these are only tufts of feathers that serve no known purpose—unless for camouflage. I do think they give him a look of distinction.

The great horned male helps feed the young. Both parents defend their fledglings against all comers, including humans, even after the owlets leave their nest.

There is something wild and mysterious about owls. I've always enjoyed seeing or hearing them in the woods. To me, owls are a splendid symbol of dark forests, fulfilling their predatory niche in nature's scheme.

14 Feathered Friends

Come, fill the Cup, and in the fire of Spring
The Winter garment of Repentance fling:
The Bird of Time has but a little way
To fly—and Lo! the Bird is on the wing.
Edward FitzGerald

Spring drags its feet in the North, but the earliest-arriving birds were already staking territorial claims. Budding new leaves turned the crowns of trees into frizzy, soft greens.

My notes read:

"Today April played mischief with the returning birds. In mid-morning, fluffy, oversized snowflakes coasted down to turn the ground white again. The orange breast of a robin brightened the scene. Ignoring spring's temporary rebuff, he cocked his eye expectantly at the snow-covered turf; the robin showed faith.

"Two or three finches pecked at leaves in the camp clearing, hoping to find a tasty tidbit. Attracted by the activity, half a dozen juncos dropped in to share the wealth—if anything turned up to share. More of their kind arrived, and it became a minor convention of tiny slate-gray suits. The tidy little birds' toothpick-thin legs were lost in the snow as they hopped around, flipping over brown leaves with their bills. Then a flurry of wind scattered snowflakes, twigs, and leaves, sending the birds en masse to the trees for safety."

In the eyes of some, snow is prettiest in the spring when it can't last long. This time, it melted away by noon.

I relaxed on my camp chair to savor the awakening. A pileated woodpecker drifted in to hammer on a dead tree, and at close range, I realized how fully this largest of the species dwarfs other woodpeckers. His black, red, and white plumage contrasted sharply with the budding leaves. The handsome bird soon wickered away to another tree, doing his part to keep the woods healthy.

125

A rose-breasted grosbeak declared to the world that this was his domain. I marveled at the rich and clear-voiced variety of notes he warbled—one of the prettiest of bird songs. Some of his melody reminded me of an oriole, robin, or thrush, and I suspected him of being part mimic. (Or was *his* song being copied?) Both male and female rose-breasted grosbeaks are singers; they even perform while incubating eggs. And very few other birds sing at night, as grosbeaks sometimes do.

High overhead, a lovesick woodcock circled endlessly, voicing its shrill mating call. I wandered across the wild hay meadow to look at the garden, and there a reddish knob of rhubarb, wrapped in crinkled green, had begun to unfurl through the soil.

My approach startled a robin, and she left her nest on one of the double corner fence posts to chirp indignantly from a nearby branch. There were four blue eggs.

I followed the path to the round pond to watch a betrothed pair of goldeneyes, their shapes mirrored by the placid water. A thick growth of black willow covered the pond banks, and the sweet perfume of pussy willows filled the air.

The wind surrendered its strength at dusk, easing the danger of sparks from my chimney at night. The evening serenade began: trilling of countless frogs, punctuated by the hoarse squawk of a lonely wood duck, the ceaseless, piercing notes of a timberdoodle circling overhead in the waning light, a lonesome owl hooting deep in the woods. . .

Twilight came on as the most peaceful time of day; even the wind slowed down to catch its breath. In the distance I heard the melancholy call of a loon. To me, this warbling, fluted call is the essence of wilderness. But being solitary creatures, loons need a good-sized body of water to patrol, and these beaver ponds would probably never suit them.

All sorts of songbirds intermix in the foliage around camp. In the variety there is always a catbird in residence to challenge my presence. The dark gray bird calls derisively from the bushes where he secretively flits about.

This member of the mockingbird family is a jester—some say a "Jekyll and Hyde" personality, though I have no such evidence. In his favor, the catbird is adroit at catching insects.

His slurring, catlike call is most commonly recognized. And yet few but the initiated are aware of his singing talent. The catbird is one of our finest songsters, with a glorious long melody. He is an excellent mimic, and you may detect other songbirds' phrases in the catbird's delivery. At times, I've been fooled into thinking the melody came from a robin or a grosbeak.

A rash of articles about the scarcity of bluebirds steered me into building a few birdhouses for them. The consensus was that there had been a ninety percent drop in the population of Eastern bluebirds; they were now on the list of endangered species.

I hung one birdhouse on the back fence at home. The others might have better odds of enticing the rare birds to the wild 80.

Ideally, bluebird houses should be placed at least two hundred yards apart. For best results in attracting bluebirds, a "trail" of nesting sites should be established. Some people set up a hundred or more houses, well spaced along country roads.

The first time I looked inside one of the bluebird houses, it was occupied—by a black-capped chickadee. The petite mother-to-be had built her nest without drawing my attention. If a bluebird was too much to expect, I'd be happy to settle for a friendly chickadee.

Recently, in a statewide poll to find Minnesotans' favorite bird, the chickadee took top honors. It is a pleasure to have these active, ever-cheery birds around, but chickadees do us an added favor—they are specialists at decimating cankerworm moths and their eggs. And as a further bonus to those who live in the snowbelt, chickadees are year-round residents. Even a snowstorm does not dampen their jolly spirit.

All you need to become entranced by chickadees is to have one of the dressy little birds land on the visor of your cap. He'll lower his head and tilt it to one side, calling softly as he studies your face.

In the cold months, I keep a supply of sunflower seeds outside my studio window to attract them. So lively and good-spirited are the little fellows, what would the long winters be like without chickadees?

The ponds were high in May, and the trill of red-winged blackbirds filled the air. Mallards and woodcock added to the happy chorus.

A robin had built her nest above the shack door. Each time I was away, the mother came back to keep her three eggs warm; but every time I opened the door, she flew off again.

A sedate pair of flycatchers flitted around the shack. The male bird paused once, in uncharacteristic flurry, to attack his image in the west window. These were probably the same birds from the year before. I've come to expect flycatchers around camp. During the summer, I like to watch them snap up insects in midair—they are welcome to all they can put away.

The dusky flycatcher (or phoebe) is the first of its kind to return from the South, even though March offers them a skimpy menu. On the backside corner of the shack, the phoebes had fashioned their usual nest of mud and moss, a very trim affair. Nooks and crannies of buildings appeal to these early arrivals for nesting sites, and they flattered me by taking up residence.

A demure brown thrasher quietly examined every bush between the ponds and camp for a potential homesite. Birds enjoy much shopping about for the perfect domicile. In the bird world, it is often customary for the male to select a nesting place. He gambles on his lady love's approval.

In springtime, birds of the same species clash over territory in twittering aerial contests; yet never have I seen any sign of injury inflicted by such squabbling. Hardly a feather is lost in these brief skirmishes. One bird always turns up dominant, and the loser silently flits away to look for unchallenged privacy.

In the afternoon, an odd sound repeated itself from the flooded meadow south of the shack. To satisfy my curiosity, I climbed onto the roof for a better view. At first I saw nothing, but when I heard the peculiar call again, there it was—an American bittern.

This was a rare privilege, because even Thoreau knew the secretive bittern mainly by voice. Sighting the shy bird is not unusual in these parts—nor, for that matter, is hearing its call at times. But it is most difficult to get close enough to *see and hear* the combined effect. The bittern—known also as marsh hen, stake driver, and bog pumper—is not nocturnal, but it makes long journeys under cover of darkness.

128

Now the freckled bittern stood motionless in the marsh grass, its head held erect, and its sharp beak pointed skyward. Suddenly it gulped in air and convulsed into a booming "pump-uh-GLOOK." It is a sound you won't forget.

A cool wind blew in from the north to sweep the sky clear. For a day in early May, the weather switch didn't surprise me, because in this climate a twenty-four-hour temperature change of fifty degrees is not uncommon.

Halfway along the ridge I picked a stump in the sun, out of the wind. It gave me a rewarding view of the island and beaver-flooded slough below. Pairs of mallards cruised the sheltered waters, studying weedbeds. Now and then a frivolous gust of wind creased its way across the surface of the backwater.

When I closed my eyes to listen to the wind in the trees, the air smelled like autumn, brisk and clean. But then I gazed on blooming trillium all around me, and felt pleasantly reassured by the jubilant reality of spring. Open woods on this high ground allowed enough sunlight for the early bloomers to flourish, in a sea of bright green, dotted with white blossoms. An expansive display of the three-petaled flowers swayed to and fro, continually bobbing and righting themselves, perfectly choreographed by the wind.

During the winter, deer and snowshoes had feasted on our three hundred young Norway pines. The lower half acre of white spruce looked fine. A doe wandered out the far side of the plantation, showing no sign of alarm.

At this time of year, the owls were hooting night or day. One owl (probably the barred owl) uttered a long, eerie, laughing sound I had never heard before. Its crazy cackle reverberated through the solemn woods, sounding for all the world like a caged, demented human. If it hadn't been broad daylight, I might have been tempted to run for shelter.

On my return to camp, a goldeneye flew out of the duck house. I wished her better luck than befell the previous tenant.

One of the continuing problems in transporting gear from home to the hinterlands is that of forgetting essentials. Mealtime came, and I realized what I had forgotten to bring this time—dishes. One cup and a spoon turned up in the shack, somewhat limiting my gourmet plans.

The wild creatures wouldn't care if I ate with my fingers, but just in case, I went out to the pickup to see if I'd missed any utensils.

Beside the truck door, a crumpled brown thrasher lay dead on the ground. The bird must have flown headlong into the window, or the sideview mirror.

It was time to check the bluebird house fastened to the back side of the tree farm sign. A swallow peeked out of the hole, and then flew up to join her mate on the overhead electric line.

Normally, tree swallows nest in old woodpecker holes, or in decaying fenceposts. These streamlined birds like to be near water, where they can circle aloft or deftly swoop to skim the surface for insects.

Both swallows kept vigil while I looked inside their home. The nest held half a dozen creamy white eggs.

The following year, the swallows had competition. At first I couldn't believe my good fortune. A swallow swooped down to examine the birdhouse, and was quickly chased away by a male bluebird! I stayed in the shadows and waited to see if my eyes were deceiving me. A not-quite-as-blue female came out of the house and joined her mate. He stood guard on an oak limb a few yards away. She returned to decide whether or not the apartment would be suitable. And while she was away, *he* went in for a look-see. The pair even drove off a blackbird that happened to land nearby.

Not that I minded the swallows' use of the bluebird house—they are sleek birds to have around. But with such a rare species as bluebirds on the scene, I tilted in their favor.

Later that second spring, I had to examine the nest to see who won, the bluebirds or the swallows. I tipped back the hinged top to peek inside, and the gaping mouths of four tiny bluebirds stretched up from the nest. They had begun to sprout feathers with faint tinges of blue, but the baby birds were still in the homely stage. I rehooked the lid and backed away, knowing their parents much be watching. Yes—looking around, I saw both bluebirds waiting anxiously for me to leave.

Toward evening, camera in hand, I crouched in the willows on the pond bank, waiting for a beaver to plug a hole in the dam. At sunset, a beaver swam toward the flowing gap; but he saw me and *ba-loop,* slid underneath the surface. As another one swam past, a hooded merganser landed on the pond ahead of him. The bird squawked and lifted off to come down in the beaver's wake. When the beaver's ripples smoothed out, the merganser's profile mirrored nicely on the water. His body was half submerged, but the diving duck's pointed bill and dashing topknot made a striking silhouette.

I'm sure the merganser found a good life in the ponds and backwaters, with minnows, mollusks, and water insects to feed on—plus the aquatic plants.

In the morning, I propped the door open to air out the shack, and a house wren flew in to join me. I was delighted to have the charming little visitor inside for close observation. As soon as I eased the door shut, the bird flew into the window screen, without injury.

For a few minutes, I watched the tiny bird as it examined nooks and crannies. Once the wren flew down to the floor and hopped along as if seeking food, or nesting material. It did not act overly frightened with me there, and I studied the bird from as close as three feet before it would move aside.

After awhile, the wren perched on the campstove shelf with its pointed bill hanging open, possibly from fear of confinement. Much as I enjoyed studying the tiny feathered guest, I quickly opened the door to freedom. Instead of flying out the door, the wren again fluttered into the window screen. I caught it as carefully as possible, and held the mite of a bird in my hands for a few seconds. Its feathers felt like silk or satin.

The wren was no bigger than my thumb, but mighty in its bubbly song. Under the circumstances, of course, this one kept silent.

I released the wren in the open doorway, and it quietly flew away.

A buzzing sound led me into the undergrowth, and I traced it to a hummingbird darting to and from blossoming moose willow. What speed! No other bird can shift its angle of flight so rapidly. This was a female rubythroat, with typical dun-green back and off-white underside. She lacked the bright red-orange throat of the male of the species.

I had not seen one of these tiniest of birds since the summer day when I stopped by the 80 on a trip farther north. That time I watched a male rubythroat as he hovered over a wildflower to draw in nectar.

How nice, I thought at the time, that the zippy little creature had timed his visit to coincide with mine. Of course, he came from a far greater distance. Hummingbirds—tropically oriented—are known to winter in Mexico, and as far south as Panama.

Rubythroats are the only species of hummingbird found in the eastern half of the United States. I marvel at this wee bird's ability to fly nonstop across the Gulf of Mexico. It is only about three-and-a-half inches long, including tail feathers, and weighs next to nothing.

Cameras with high-speed lenses have recorded the hummingbird's amazing oscillating wingbeat patterns. No wonder they hum so audibly. To the naked eye, their wings are a constant blur. As you watch one of the little tropical jewels, even the female's plumage changes color rapidly, depending upon the constantly shifting angle of light.

Hummingbirds show no fear of humans, and they will take nectar from a hand-held flower if it is to their taste.

To casual observers, the hawkmoth (or sphinx) is often confused with the hummingbird. They do make similar humming sounds. Although the hawk moth's nectar-gathering technique is much the same, this nonbird is decorated only in a mixture of blotched browns. You may have seen one of these odd moths over flower beds after sundown. (They often visit my petunias at that time of day.)

The female rubythroat builds her dainty nest from soft plant fibers and spider webs. The male posts guard. Then she covers her nest with bits of moss and lichen for a superb camouflage. Her saliva glues the nest into position under a tree limb. There the mother hummingbird deposits two infinitesimal plain white eggs—all the nest will hold. One protruding leaf above the nest is enough to furnish a substantial roof.

This little gem of a bird has an extensile brush-tipped tongue that rolls into a tiny tube for sucking up nectar. It also eats very small insects, along with the diet of nectar, and feeds aphids and such to its young. This is done by forcible throat injection—not very attractive to us, but lifegiving fluid for the baby hummingbirds.

My peewee visitor from Central America suddenly hummed out of sight, vanishing like a will-o'-the-wisp.

"What is so rare as a day in June?" With the day's transplanting completed, I plunked down on the camp chair to rest.

On this vibrant summer day, fleecy white clouds sailed across the sky. Their forms constantly shifted in high winds, and their cotton-like fringes dissipated as they traveled. In a whimsical mood, I pulled a pencil stub from my shirt pocket and scrawled these lines on the back of a paper plate:

> I don't see why
> The clouds should race
> Across the sky—
> They'll never spy
> A better place
> No matter how they try.

Waving grasses undulated in the wind, and as I gazed idly at the wild hay meadow, an indigo bunting fluttered down to feed on the stalk tips. After all, at three in the afternoon, it was teatime.

I took note of the bird's technique. He landed on a stem of his choosing and rode the slender stalk till it bowed down to a fairly level position. Only that way could he reach the seeds. The almost weightless bird bobbed up and down with the wind, picking daintily at his meal. Again at 6:00 P.M. (the dinner hour), the blue-feathered bird returned to feed in the same place. And once more at dusk, for a bedtime snack. This time a goldfinch settled in to copy the bunting's style; the two birds never acknowledged each other's presence.

Just before dark, a flurry of agitated birds disturbed the evening hush. Three or four burly robins, joined by a smaller bird, ganged up to chase away a lone blue jay. He had probably been caught raiding a nest. The robins chirped in clamorous disgust, and dove upon the jay without mercy. He squawked in alarmed defiance and left hurriedly for a friendlier neighborhood.

Peace reigned again.

15 A Squirrel's World

*. . . and the silent energy of nature stirred the soul to its
inmost depths.*
Thomas Cole

Meeting a wild animal in its natural habitat is always exciting to me,
but for everyday entertainment, I give high marks to squirrels. The
frolicking of a squirrel enlivens any landscape; I'm impressed by that
jaunty, devil-may-care leap to land on a flimsy limb. And deep in a
lonely winter woods, often there is no other sound to share but the
rasping complaint of a squirrel when a "trespasser" comes along.

In the backwoods on a spring day, I came upon an unsophisticated
gray squirrel. I happened to have a few black walnuts in my pocket,
because to my knowledge there were no walnut trees for miles
around, and I intended to plant a few. I tossed an unhusked walnut to
the squirrel on the ground to see if he would recognize it as food. At
first he ignored my offering; then the sharp fragrance of walnut
crossed his nostrils, and he picked up the nut and began to bite off the
outer husk. Whether he reacted to instinct, smell, or just curiosity, I
could only guess.

After dismantling the husk, the squirrel quietly departed with the
whole walnut in his teeth. I wondered if he preferred to eat it in
private, or would hide it. If he did bury the nut, and never found it
again, a walnut tree might take root on that hillside. And years later,
the tree could begin to feed succeeding generations of squirrels.

Surely our forests would be less prosperous without the busyness
of squirrels. Thanks to their feverish habit of burying nuts in autumn,
squirrels plant countless trees every year, because they hide more
nuts than they find. Even if, as claimed in a recent study, some 85
percent of those nuts are retrieved in winter, the remaining 15

percent represents an awesome amount of new growth nationwide. No other animal contributes as much toward propagation of oak, walnut, and hickory—plus pine and spruce trees.

Still, to some people a squirrel is just another pesky rodent. Not everyone can tolerate the wiry little bounder's bird-feeder piracy. As anyone who feeds birds soon discovers, squirrels are ingenious at gaining access to forbidden feeders. To foil the freebooters, I once tried placing the seed mix in a box on top of a T-shaped iron clothesline post. The first gray squirrel to come along attempted to scale the post, and failed. With no claw grip on the hard surface, he kept sliding back down. After a while he wised up and bent his paws inward to *shinny* up on his wrists.

Next, I hung the feeder from the clothesline, safely off the ground and away from the iron post. I knew a nearby tree might provide access, but no squirrel could get a claw hold on the wire clothesline. They tried, but always lost their grip on the post or wire.

One squirrel persisted. Finally, on the umpteenth attempt, he went higher up the tree, gauged distance, and launched himself through the air. That tenacious upstart hit the clothesline and spun around like a whirligig, but he got a toehold on the wooden goody box. I didn't have the heart to chase him off. (To maintain a feeder exclusively for birds, nothing beats the traditional tall steel post with a metal shield below the seed tray.)

In order to ease winter feeding competition between birds and squirrels in my yard, I now hang an ear of field corn from a tree trunk. To enforce sharing, I shove a nail into the pulpy center at each end of the cob, and suspend the corn ear on a wire.

Beyond the mainstay of acorns, squirrels enjoy sunflower seed handouts, and they are notoriously partial to peanut butter. Although squirrels nibble on leaf buds in all seasons, they like a variety of fruits, nuts, and seeds; the rascals sometimes sample my green tomatoes. And in the wild, squirrels are very fond of mushrooms, which they store off the ground.

Some friends of mine, both avid bird watchers, are antisquirrel. Their suburban yard is dominated by huge oak trees, and every fall they live-trap and transport squirrels religiously; then they rake up bushels of acorns for the trash man to haul away.

If you do live-trap squirrels for transfer, be aware: they cannot survive the stress of captivity in a small enclosure for very long. After a few hours of close confinement, a squirrel will die of shock.

As with most anything wild, squirrels suffer constant predation. From the air they are meal targets for owls and hawks. And on the ground lurk weasels, foxes, coyotes, and the occasional bobcat or lynx. Also, the arboreal pine marten pursues and captures squirrels in the treetops. Furthermore, cats and dogs take their toll of squirrels, as do road vehicles. But despite all of these hazards, plus hunting pressure, the bushytails manage to hold their own.

Technically, the common Minnesota gopher is classified as "the 13-lined ground squirrel." Of the four tree-climbing species native to the state, the fox squirrel is largest in size, followed by the gray, red, and flying squirrels. Occasionally the gray and red squirrels come into conflict over territory, and you still hear the myth that red squirrels castrate male grays to cut down competition. When gray squirrels invade the realm of red squirrels, the zippy, smaller reds will drive them off, but that is all.

Viewed from my studio window, one sprightly red squirrel can brighten a drab winter day. Even at ten below zero he shows up for a free meal of field corn. Though only about half the size of his cousins, the little red will chase off two or three gray squirrels to guard "his" ear of corn. This particular squirrel eats only the soft inner kernel of corn, whereas the grays eat the whole kernel. Sometimes the little red will tolerate a gray on the ground, feeding on his leftovers.

At times—having eaten his fill—the energetic red is seized by the urge to store food. Clocking four or five twenty-foot trips per minute, he beats a narrow path through the snow from the tree to a nearby hiding place. Since a squirrel lacks the cheek pouches of a chipmunk, he carries only one kernel at a time. You'd think he'd burn more energy in storage activity than could ever be reclaimed.

The nocturnal so-called flying squirrels are seldom seen, because they feed at night and hole up in daylight hours. If you are lucky and know where they live, you may spot one venturing forth toward dusk. Those large, glassy eyes are unforgettable.

The flying squirrel has drab back fur, soft and dense, tinged with russet, and its underside is white. Although this small squirrel cannot actually fly, it is a superb glider. The tail serves as a rudder for guiding direction. A thin web of folded skin attached to fore and hind legs on both sides looks like a poorly fitted coat. But when flight becomes necessary, this extra skin stretches out flat for a parachute effect. The flying squirrel simply spreads all four legs and sails away.

Toward sundown one day, the boys and I had pitched the tent, and we needed campfire wood; a hollow, barkless derelict of a tree looked fine for the purpose. It stood about fifteen feet tall, and no boy with a hatchet can resist such a challenge. I used to harbor the same weakness, until I came to understand the value of den trees for wildlife. More than sixty species of birds and animals depend upon dead trees, which foresters call "snags," for a home. Game managers recommend saving a few in cutover plots.

When my young son Alan began to hack at the dry tree trunk, two flying squirrels scrambled out of a woodpecker hole and perched atop the jagged shell. We stopped in our tracks to study them while those baby-doll eyes fixed on the threat below.

Suddenly one flying squirrel spread its legs, batlike, and descended in a graceful glide, swinging upward in the final few feet to clutch a nearby treetrunk. The other little squirrel followed suit, and we stood transfixed by the beauty of it all.

Any squirrel makes travel in the trees look easy; to him the treetops are an aerial highway. Acrobatics are his way of life, and amazing high-wire acts are just routine.

When you watch a pair of gray squirrels spiraling around a treetrunk, you'll notice that *up* or *down* makes no difference in their speed. Unlike a raccoon, for instance, which most often chooses to descend slowly, backside first, a squirrel can race down head first, with hind feet turned to grip the bark.

It's the dashing tail that accentuates a squirrel's character. For one thing, it doubles his size. When disturbed, he flaunts his tail expressively, twitching it herky-jerky as he scolds you from an overhead branch. Perched on a barren winter limb, a squirrel uses that long-haired sweep over his back to ward off the wind. And when he is curled up in a nest or den, he needs an extra buffer against the cold. Moreover, a squirrel's tail is crucial for balance.

Once in awhile you will see a squirrel with only half a tail, the result of a close call. (Some naturalists suspect that another squirrel has nipped it off, but no one has witnessed the act.) There is one such squirrel in our neighborhood now—a pitiful sight, but the loss doesn't seem to limit its activities.

We have a peculiar squirrel around camp. He's a gray, but his tail—and tail only—is a *strawberry blonde*. One day last summer this two-tone squirrel crept into the clearing to examine a frizzy foot-long strand of rope on the ground. To my amusement, he began to wrestle with the rope. Then he tossed it into the air and rolled onto his back to catch it with all four paws. This act he repeated several times. He rolled and tumbled like a cat toying with a victim. When the novelty wore off, he bounced away.

The melanistic examples I've encountered have most often been of the gray variety. At one time there was a family of five or six black squirrels in a yard I passed on my way to work each morning. Their activity appeared to be normal, but that all-black pelage struck me as dangerously poor camouflage against predators. As for the opposite, albino squirrels, they occur less often than blacks, at least in my experience.

In the process of painting my house last year, I stood a ladder against the peak within reach of a tall balsam fir. An alarmed squirrel sounded immediate disapproval; as I soon learned, she had a nest of young in that tree. After chattering at me for awhile, the mother squirrel went quiet and began to move her babies. Gently, one by one, she clamped each tiny squirrel in her mouth and moved it down through layered branches, then up into my neighbor's spruce. Considerable legwork, and unnecessary, but that maternal instinct . . .

Somehow, squirrels convey a spirit of adventure. I recall one summer day on Lake Koronis near Paynesville, Minnesota. The outboard motor was buzzing my boat across the ripples when I spotted a muskrat up ahead—in the middle of the lake? I pulled alongside the swimming . . . *squirrel,* not muskrat! He was merrily paddling his way toward the far shore, something like half a mile to go. And unless a big northern pike or snapping turtle waylaid the spunky little explorer, I'll bet he made his destination.

During construction of the fifty-seven-story IDS Tower in downtown Minneapolis, three citified squirrels took up residence. They stayed for several months, climbing higher as the building progressed. Admiring workmen fed them daily. Said one man, "It gets lonely up there."

A representative of the Animal Humane Society set live traps—on the *fifty-second floor*. But not even crunchy peanut butter could entice those squirrels into leaving their "penthouse."

In that same area another time, I went for a noon-hour stroll down Nicollet Mall. Was that a squirrel nest in one of the small trees? Sure enough, as people paraded by on the sidewalk, a squirrel scurried up the tree and climbed into its nest.

I weighed the incongruity. Any squirrel would have to negotiate several blocks of heavy traffic (even from the closest park) to reach this tree in the heart of the city. And what could he find to eat? Across the street, a gaudy popcorn wagon dispensed its tantalizing aroma. The sagacious squirrel could count on a steady supply of popcorn being spilled on the sidewalk.

Not long after that special tree shed its leaves, the highly conspicuous nest disappeared, and so did the squirrel. Now the tree was festooned with Christmas lights. I missed the rambunctious symbol of freedom. In a mercenary atmosphere of concrete and steel, that squirrel had given me a link to the wild world. But one saucy squirrel's effort to integrate with humans had come to an end.

16 The Wily Weasel

To slowly trace the forest's shady scene, where things that
own not man's dominion dwell . . .
Lord Byron

Tending a tree farm is a labor of love, but there is a bonus—the chance to observe wildlife in a natural setting. Sooner or later you're apt to encounter anything from a bear on down to our smallest carnivore, the weasel.

Beavers had drowned an acre of hardwoods on the slough island, and several cords of firewood could be salvaged—ash, oak, elm, and maple. With snow on the ground, it's always comforting to see a stack of dry wood ready for the stove.

Toward sundown on a brisk December day, I shut off the chain saw and welcomed silence. As I pulled on a heavier jacket, a strange crackling noise came from beyond a bend in the rough road that crosses the island. The spasmodic clattering puzzled me until I eased closer. Ruffed grouse were feeding in thick clumps of alder, and their movements rattled frozen branches. One bird edged out on a limb and stretched his neck to clamp his beak onto a cone. The branch sagged, and with a flurry of beating wings, he regained his balance. Two more grouse were taking on their evening meal in the same resolute fashion.

Of necessity, I had to pass by their supper table on my way back to camp. Three or four grouse roared out of the alders and crossed the slough to shelter in the main woods.

When I approached the shack, a silent ghost bounded across the clearing. The snowshoe hare left wide tracks and disappeared.

The shack looked inviting, but my camp supply of split wood was low, and winter days aren't long enough. After piling up wood for the night, I sat down on a rustic camp chair to catch my breath. The late afternoon sun broke through winter clouds, and tall aspen trunks glowed in chartreuse-gold. Along the western horizon of bare tree-tops, the sky would soon transform into a purple and orange sunset.

While I sat there admiring the sky's changing colors, a cautious weasel peeked out from behind the camp table to my left. His creamy white coat was nearly complete for winter camouflage—a lingering brown streak remained on his back.

He was after leftovers from a rabbit I had cleaned that morning. The weasel's nostrils flared at the smell of blood, and his ebony eyes studied scraps in the snow. He seized a piece of raw meat and sampled it, then he bit off a chunk and disappeared into a pile of brush I had planned to burn.

In a semicircle of meat-packing trips, the weasel moved goodies to various hiding places, always hurrying back for more. He took long strips of rabbit fur to warm his den—or the skin would be edible in a pinch.

If I moved slightly to watch his progress, he dropped the loot and zipped for cover. There he waited a second or two before leaping toward the meat scraps again. In that distinctive weasel manner, his tubular body arched in sinuous rhythm as he looped swiftly across the snow. His triangular head and long neck gave him a serpentine appearance.

Weasel tracks soon radiated in every direction from the camp table. Some of his routes were direct, and some were devious. Like a jack-in-the-box, he popped up through the snow in unexpected places and looked pertly at me.

Although adult short-tailed weasels (as I judged this one to be) weigh only about four ounces, they have something in common with big cats; they are capable of carrying off prey that far outweighs them.

The head of the snowshoe hare surely outweighed the little weasel. I watched him tug and pull and drop it. His lithe body stretched and twisted as he circled the problem. There had to be a way to salvage this prize hunk of food.

Tenaciously, the weasel began to push the rabbit head through powdery snow. His streamlined body moved in short bursts, shoving like a miniature bulldozer, but he soon gave that up as too slow.

Next he tried pulling the head; it immediately snagged between two thick sprouts. Back to pushing. No progress. At last he clamped his teeth into the head and wiggled it free. With Herculean effort, the weasel managed to carry off his prize—a comical sight, with those long rabbit ears dragging in the snow.

This choice portion went under a pile of bark slabs, and it took longer to get the load safely hidden. In fact, I had about given up on his returning for more, but he wasn't finished yet. Occasionally he dashed over to check me out. If I didn't move, he went about his business. The black-tipped tail pointed jauntily skyward on trip after trip.

The sun was setting, and the enterprising weasel had most of the rabbit scraps tucked away. I left the outdoor chair to get my camera for a sunset picture and went back inside.

When I glanced out at the table again, the weasel was on top, after the liver. With this delicacy in his teeth, he jumped into the three-inch hole in the round table's center support. Abruptly his head appeared again.

I went out to see what his reaction might be. Ever cautious, he ducked out of sight. A bit of mischief came over me, and I covered the hole with loose snow and stood back. *Ploop!* The weasel's head popped up through the snow. His dark eyes fixed me with a smoldering stare. I moved, and he ducked, leaving a perfectly round, golfball size hole in the snow.

I set an empty beer can over the hole. Rustling came from underneath, and the can tilted. He pushed the can off at an angle and glared up at me. I stepped back, and the weasel came out to give the beer can a long, curious sniff.

I had to smile as I went into the shack to light the gas lantern. When I came out for an armload of firewood, the weasel ran up to examine my boots. (More meat on the hoof?) When I bent down, he bounded for cover.

By now it was getting dark and turning colder; time to cook supper and call it a day.

Any weasel is a tireless hunter; often it seems to kill merely for sport, leaving dead bodies untouched. Farmers who keep chickens see the tiny predator as a bloodthirsty assassin. In one night's rampage, they'll tell you, a single weasel can kill twenty-five or thirty hens in wanton waste. In such cases, a long-tailed weasel is the most likely culprit; short-tailed weasels seldom prey on poultry larger than a chick.

Naturalist Ernest Thompson Seton once observed a weasel clinging to a fleeing rabbit; the attacker's teeth gripped the victim's neck, and Seton claimed the weasel hung on until the rabbit collapsed.

Once on a November day in woods near Squaw Lake in northern Minnesota, I watched a weasel chase a tiny shrew through a brushpile. That weasel ignored me completely; he focused full attention on the potential meal. His white body disappeared under sticks on the far side, and the terrified shrew came out on my side near the top of the pile. There he paused to listen, nose twitching nervously. The weasel stalked him in deadly silence. Suddenly the shrew vanished into the brush again. In a flash of white, the sleek predator closed in from a new angle. Neither one appeared again.

Aided by keen eyes and sense of smell, weasels make extremely effective predators. They prefer to stalk live prey by scent, and they harbor a strong urge to store meat after a kill. To survive, a weasel must eat one-third of its weight daily. These hunters can catch ground-feeding birds, and they like eggs.

On the plus side, weasels help control small rodents. Fully half of a weasel's diet consists of mice. And during cold months, mice may be the *only* source of food. Since mice or voles can destroy young trees (apple orchards are especially vulnerable), weasels play a valuable role in holding down rodent damage.

Weasels favor woody cover along stream banks, and cleared land reverting to forest. They also like to patrol black spruce and tamarack bogs for a meal. If food is plentiful, the nimble hunter may live out its life in a small acreage; otherwise, it will travel a wide area.

The weasel is a loner. He will not tolerate another in his territory, and unless the competitor leaves, a fight to the death is inevitable. Weight counts in these battles. Being slightly smaller, females often fall victims to heavier males. Mother Nature can be harsh, but maintaining a healthy weasel population is the result.

A weasel has remarkable courage and will face up to an antagonist many times its size. Generally, its four-legged enemies are the mink, marten, fox, and coyote. Owls and hawks also dine on weasels.

Of three species of weasel native to northern North America—the long-tailed, short-tailed, and least weasel—only the latter does not sport a black-tipped tail. The black tip on the tail of the two largest weasels sometimes saves their lives. An attacking owl or hawk is more apt to focus on the black tip than on the body when pursuit is against a snowy background.

In the northern states and Canada, weasels change coats twice a year. With short-tailed weasels (*Mustela erminea,* often called ermine), the average male is about eleven inches long, and the female seldom exceeds nine inches. There is some overlap in length—a *small* long-tailed and a *large* short-tailed may be about the same size.

Weasels breed in midsummer, but due to delayed implantation, the female doesn't give birth until the following spring. A litter varies from four to thirteen young, and two months later they are hunting on their own. Individual life span is ten years at most.

Weasels use a variety of sounds to vocalize their moods. They often hiss while sniffing out prey, and purr softly when content. If excited, they'll emit a series of muted barks; if alarmed, a shrill screech in one sharp note.

Any weasel I have ever seen was either motionless or running. They appear to use only two speeds for travel—medium fast and full throttle. A leisurely stroll is not for them.

Do they never sleep? I've come upon weasels in the woods at all hours of the day or night, usually during winter. One scrambled high into an oak tree when he felt threatened by me.

Weasels are members of the family Mustelidae, animals with musk glands, like the marten, fisher, mink, otter, ferret, badger, skunk, and wolverine. When frightened or irritated, weasels discharge an offensive musky odor from two glands at the base of the tail. Their scent is not as pungently potent as that of a skunk, but it possibly serves to confuse an attacker. They probably use this musk to mark their territory. It may also aid them in attracting a mate.

In the shack one night, I was asleep in the top bunk. My dog, April, lay curled up on the bottom bunk. Along about midnight, a rustling of paper woke me. I reached for the flashlight. Under the campstove shelf, a weasel stopped his rummaging to stare up at the light. I was tired, in no mood for nonsense, and felt tempted to shoot the little scoundrel for disturbing my rest.

But logic won out—the marauder would keep the shack free of mice. I threw a candle stub at him and he quickly took cover. The black Labrador leaped out of her bed to sniff at the corner where the weasel escaped.

Around 3:00 A.M. a different noise awakened me, a rapid-fire *tat-tat-tat* on the east wall. I couldn't tell whether it came from inside or out. As soon as I turned off my flashlight, the strange tapping resumed. I'd never get back to sleep with that noise, so I got up to investigate.

There I stood in the dark, waiting for the muffled tapping to continue. When it began again, I flashed the light down between the half-finished interior board wall and the exterior plastic covering. A weasel's black eyes fixed on the light. The noise came from his nose pounding rapidly against the outer plastic sheeting. Since the smooth, flat surface didn't offer any tooth-hold, he must have felt trapped, unable to comprehend why he could see through this mysterious material that held him confined.

I dropped a stick of firewood down beside the weasel to offer him an escape ladder. That frightened him, and he gave off a musky stench. He slipped out of the enclosure and didn't return that night.

The dog, of course, took part in the excitement. I coaxed her back into bed to calm her down, and opened the door to air out the shack. When morning came, the faint smell of musk still hung in the air.

The weasel is an essential link in the forest food chain. But more than that, this tiniest of carnivores is the epitome of wildness, an intriguing symbol of the natural world.

17 A Dog To Remember

Recollect that the Almighty, who gave the dog to be com-
panion of our pleasures and our toils, hath invested him
with a nature noble and incapable of deceit.
Sir Walter Scott

We bought the black Labrador puppy in April, and that became her name. She rode up north with Alan, Nathan, and me in October for the first time.

At the shack that evening, the gangly pup went loony. She ran around nonstop, jumping on and off the beds. Her strange behavior worried us, but nothing we said or did would calm her down. Even outside, the dog circled in perpetual motion. Could it be poison? We had kept her in the car during errands in Larsville. At mealtime, the three of us tried to eat while April ran all over camp. And yet she wanted to be with us constantly, in and out of the door whenever one of us opened it. We took turns trying to console her, but food or water didn't help.

At bedtime, Alan chose the lower bunk, and at last the pup settled down, snuggled next to him in the sleeping bag. Our best guess was that the dog's hyperactivity had been due to overexcitement in the new surroundings—lots of strange animal scents and such.

Anyone who has owned a dog knows Labs are amongst the friendliest of canines. April was typical; she would lie down on my feet to be sure she was close enough. Then she would keep those soulful eyes on me until I got up, and trot along at my side. In the woods, she would never stray out of sight.

When morning came, April watched me with those pseudo-sad eyes as she struggled out of the sleeping bag. That woke Alan, and we all had breakfast. To our relief, the pup ate normally and appeared to adjust to her new locale.

The boys and dog left for a hike behind Crazy Swens's cabin to see what the ravens were croaking about over there. While they were gone, I carried a twenty-five-pound chunk of salt to the south end of the island and placed it on a low boulder for the deer. If a porcupine should find it first, he might eat the whole thing, so dearly do porkies love salt.

Alan and Nathan reported on the ravens: the big birds were scavenging the remains of rotting carcasses left by a bear baiter.

*　　*　　*

In February, the dog and I went up to supervise more bulldozing. The beaver trench below the dam on the north end of the island concerned me. What if the bulldozer bogged down? I'd never convince another operator to show up. I held my breath until the Caterpillar rolled across the ice and snow without any problem.

The pup found great sport in racing up and down the freshly plowed dirt road behind the 'dozer. Occasionally she plunged into the snow on either side to investigate tantalizing scents.

By noon, Jake had extended the road about five hundred yards to the border across from the island's south end. There my woodcutter had stacked several cords of hardwood, mostly from trees drowned above the expanded beaver dam. The dead trees were accessible for salvage only during winter months.

April and I went back to camp for lunch. Inside the shack, a red squirrel scampered out through a hole in a ceiling corner. The dog made a fruitless leap and gave one excited yelp. Impulsively, I removed the squirrel's nest. I might as well have left it for the nervy sprite, because he soon rebuilt it in the same place.

Now I knew what had been nibbling on everything. Candles, a bar of soap, the plastic lid to a glass jar of sugar—anything that smelled edible had been tested by squirrel teeth.

An hour later, I bounced over the virgin road in Jake's four-wheel-drive pickup. He needed more fuel and radiator mixture. April rode in the cab beside me, a picture of contentment.

By five o'clock a new road reached into the back 80. With darkness coming on, Jake shut off his machine and we climbed into his pickup for the ride back out of the woods.

Right after supper, the Lab and I hit the hay. I fixed her bed on the lower bunk, and she curled up to dream dog dreams.

At 3:00 A.M. I had to feed the fire. When I put the flashlight on April's dish, it exposed a tiny shrew, gorging on dog food. He scooted out of sight when the pup leaped out of bed to investigate my interest in her dish.

Snow flurries greeted us in the morning. I warmed up the car, and estimated the temperature at ten degrees below zero.

April gobbled breakfast. Dogs are not famous for dainty eating habits. At home, our tomcat still had his nose out of joint over sharing his pampered domain with—of all things—a *dawg*. The cat made a very begrudging acceptance of this insult. And when April gulped down her food, he sat there watching her uncouth behavior with a look of total disgust. The friendly pup never understood why the cat refused to play with her.

April and I traipsed back over the new road to its limit. Between uprooted trees, frozen topsoil furnished us a black roadway for easy walking. After two days of grinding 'dozer noise, it was a pleasure to stroll through quiet woods.

A porcupine, soaking up sunshine, huddled on a high tree limb, where he resembled a squirrel nest. April never knew it was up there, and thank goodness she didn't encounter one on the ground when I wasn't looking. I thought about a friend and his problem Dalmatian. While he lived up near Lake Superior, his pooch just never learned to avoid tangling with porcupines. Don spent long hours plucking quills from that foolish dog's muzzle.

Deer tracks were everywhere. During the night the whitetails had utilized our new road for a browsing bonanza. When we approached the lone pine above the conifer seedlings, five or six deer bounded off the road below the hill. I stopped, and April voiced a single "Woof!" She had never seen a deer before (that I knew of), although she must have picked up the scent.

Man and dog grabbed a nap in the shack before heading homeward.

*   *   *

In May, the wood ticks were waiting for April and me. Periodically I had to check her floppy ears.

There were days in early summer when all of us exceeded the quota of ticks. Once the boys were in competition to see who picked off the most. Those miniature pests were partial to Alan, and after he had counted and removed forty woodticks, we all gave up and stopped counting.

The name "wood" tick is a misnomer for the common brown variety. These oval arachnids lurk mainly in tall grass, weeds, and shrubs. The ugly little parasite's hard-shelled flat body is equipped with eight legs exending sidewise. Man, animals, and some birds play host to wood ticks. When any warm-blooded creature brushes past, the tick latches on unnoticed.

Furthermore, wood ticks are able to travel on the wind, the way spiders expand their range. On a summer day, standing shirtless in the open road, I have suddenly found one on my bare skin.

As with mosquitoes, only female wood ticks suck blood, since both require fluid to reproduce. Whereas the bite of a mosquito will surely get your attention, woodticks manage to do their drilling without your being aware of it. The host's blood is drawn through the tick's microscopic beak; minute recurved teeth ensure the ticks ability to cling tenaciously.

There are almost as many suggestions for removing ticks as there are cures for hiccups. People tell you to burn them off or unscrew the head (clockwise or counterclockwise?), and so on. In spite of the temptation, it is not a good idea to yank a tick off your skin. That is bad medicine, most everyone agrees, because it can leave the head's hooked beak embedded. "He'll just grow a new body and keep on sucking blood," some say. Whether or not you believe that, it is best to get them off as soon as possible to avoid potential infection.

If the tick has been anchored for awhile, put a drop of vegetable oil or gasoline on it; then the intruder will loosen its hold and come out easily. Next, wash with soapy water. The point of contact may itch for a few hours, but a sprinkling of Bactine or some such lotion has a soothing effect.

Around a campfire, the boys liked to drop a wood tick into the coals to hear the soft *sput* when the little demon headed for Hades.

As summer winds down, the supply of ticks diminishes, but they do survive winter to reemerge the following spring. It has been claimed that wood ticks can live without sustenance for as long as six years. If only we could avoid our grocery bills for that long!

Ticks are a nuisance, leaving you with an itching, unclean feeling, but in Minnesota they have been nothing to worry about. Cases of tick-carried tularemia are relatively rare here. (Actually, horseflies are the most common carrier.) In the West, tick transfer of Rocky Mountain spotted fever to humans is more prevalent.

But now we are warned of another kind of tick, *Ixodes dammini,* carrier of Lyme disease. The name comes from Lyme, Connecticut, where the malady was first recognized in this country in 1975.

The tiny pests are less than half the size of common wood ticks. Whitetail deer are the primary hosts for adult ticks of this type, and certain mice carry the larval and nymphal forms in summer. Even these minute forms can transmit the microbe, causing Lyme disease.

Both wild and domestic animals are potential carriers. Oddly, most mammals do not seem to suffer ill effects from the tick-carried spirochete. People, however, often develop a rash that expands in rings, like a bulls-eye. Victims may have symptoms that include fatigue, chills, fever, headache, and muscle or joint pain. Unless treated promptly, the patient can develop arthritis, partial paralysis, and heart problems. In cases of delayed treatment, recovery can be very slow.

Lyme disease is curable at all stages, usually with antibiotics such as penicillin or tetracycline. Still, to avoid letting the *Ixodes* tick get friendly with you, it is wise to wear a long-sleeved shirt when you're afield, and to tuck your pants legs into boot tops. Light-colored clothing makes it easier to spot the ticks. Precaution is necessary in the woods from April through October. And always use insect repellent on your socks and slacks; diethyl-toluamide (DEET) discourages tick attachment, but it does not *kill* ticks, it merely repels them.

Only recently has a chemical proved reliable for killing ticks, chiggers, and mosquitoes—*Permanone,* with permethrin as its active ingredient, kills ticks on contact. It is not recommended for use on your skin, but it is nontoxic and it's biodegradable. Sprayed on clothing, the chemical will kill ticks for up to twelve hours.

Although the U.S. Environmental Protection Agency sanctions use of permethrin in various pesticide products, each state must grant approval. First developed for the military, Permanone Tick Repellent is rapidly gaining recognition as a safeguard against the Lyme disease tick.

There is also available a dip and a rub for dogs and horses. Already legal in all fifty states, Perma-Kill Tick, Flea, & Lice Killer for Dogs can be purchased in various sporting goods stores. It is odorless, and effective for up to twenty-four hours.

Lyme disease is spreading throughout the United States, and to other countries. The tiny ticks have even been found on migrating birds. Several counties in Minnesota have recorded cases of *Ixodes* tick infection, and our northern county is one having the dubious distinction. Hereafter we'll have to be more careful during the warm months.

*   *   *

April bounded exuberantly through the woods, never far away. Once I teased her by hiding behind a tree. When she realized that I was not in sight, she stretched her neck high to look around. "I'm lost!" must have crossed the dog's mind. She started to whimper, and suddenly leaped away in the wrong direction. "April!" I called, and she raced toward me, almost wagging her tail off with joy. We both sat down for a happy reunion, and I never teased her that way again.

The next day I launched another planting binge: two wild grapevines, a few test-case blueberry bushes from a different county, bittersweet vine, and a small mountain ash tree transported from the shores of Lake Superior, where they are abundant. If there is a good crop of mountain ash berries in northern Minnesota, some robins will spend the winter there. (The fruit is palatable to birds only after alternate freezing and thawing.) One of these trees would not guarantee me any winter robins, but it is a hardy and beautiful tree to add to the landscape.

April became bored with my planting spree; she much preferred to play. When I took off a glove and laid it down, she clamped it between her teeth and sassily trotted away. If I didn't know better, I'd swear that dog was smiling. I threatened and cajoled, but she would not bring the glove back. When I approached her, she picked it up again and dodged away from me. I accepted defeat and went about my work. After I ignored her, the little imp came back wagging her tail—but without the glove. (It turned up later.)

This exhibition of April's mischief reminded me of the pigeon incident at home. When the kiddies were quite small, we lived not far from Minnehaha Creek. During the summer, our yard never lacked a tubful of crayfish, minnows, and turtles. We had a cat then, but no dog. Gail had an insatiable craving for pets, and she branched out with rabbits. Yes, they multiplied. She and her girl friend saw to that by clandestinely arranging a rabbit romance. If we parents hadn't put our collective feet down, we'd have been knee-deep in rabbits.

"But they're all so kee-yoo-oot!" Gail explained.

The pendulum of her interest swung over to birds. Although our pet crow already contributed spice to the menagerie, he was not friendly enough for Gail. One day she climbed up under a trestle and came home with a baby pigeon. "His name is Baby," she announced.

When we moved farther out in the suburbs, Gail brought the bird along, and shortly thereafter we acquired the puppy. April never picked a fight with anyone or anything. Nevertheless, that pigeon took delight in attacking the dog at every opportunity. The fool bird puffed up his chest feathers pompously, cooed a gutteral pigeon version of "Charge!" and flew at the congenial pup. It may have had something to do with territorial rights. He would land on the dog's back, seize a hair in his beak, and try to yank it loose.

Baby often fluttered down from the roof to run around under the dog's feet, pecking at her legs and underside. April simply viewed the bird's unorthodox behavior as a game, an amusing pastime. And occasionally she succeeded in clamping her soft mouth over the pigeon. With the bird in her mouth and her head held high, the Lab pranced triumphantly away. Of course we quickly intervened before any harm could be done.

When this happened, Gail severely scolded April and anyone in sight who may have allowed the conflict. The pigeon always came away unscathed—and uneducated. That coo-coo bird never gave up picking on April; the dog took it all in stride.

There came a day when I was working in the garden. The pigeon floated down to peck seeds at my feet, and he bobbed and strutted "prr-coo, prr-coo" in delight with these newfound delicacies. Most pets thrive on attention, and since I was occupied, he flew back into the lawn toolshed—his private retreat.

A short time later, a big dog moseyed through our backyard. April was nowhere in sight. The stray dog moved on while I concentrated on my digging.

Abruptly, I heard a fluttering of wings and looked up to see the pigeon flying against the inside of the shed window facing the garden. I never gave him much credit for sense, but even he knew better than that. Suddenly it hit me—that big dog was after the bird! I hurried around to the shed entrance. Too late—the stray dog ran off with the pigeon in his mouth. I threw a rock at the mutt, and he dropped the crumpled bird. There was nothing I could do, and that night I had to break the bad news to a tearful Gail.

Back to my planting project—now April came over to watch me dig a hole, and tried to show me how it *should* be done. After setting in two more apple trees in a clearing by the garden—a Northern Greening and my favorite, Prairie Spy—I went for a walk with the dog.

Our beaver family had abandoned their original lodge near camp; I went down to the lower end of the island, where they had settled in a new home. Some of the stacks of firewood cut in February stood precariously close to water's edge. The woodpiles would be safe from flooding only if those energetic rodents didn't raise the dam too high.

On this trip north, I had the boat along; by midafternoon April and I were cruising on a nearby lake. The dog had been *in* lakes before; typical of a Labrador, she thoroughly enjoyed swimming out after tossed sticks. But riding in a boat was a new experience for her.

When I pulled into a bay, I was tempted to cast a plug for bass, but no doubt she would jump in after it. Then I'd have to row in to shore to get her back into the boat. I tried bobber fishing for a few minutes.

April wouldn't sit still for that; she kept rocking the boat. Fishing with the dog along was out of the question, so I started the outboard motor and we bounced across the waves. April sat proudly in the bow, with her ears trailing in the wind.

Tall pines on an island in that lake had always intrigued me. The big trees must have survived lumberjack days because of their inaccessible location. Either the state or county owned the island and today I'd go out there and measure those trees.

At four and one-half feet off the ground, one of the pines read eight feet, one inch, in circumference. (The state record is nine feet eight inches.) I couldn't measure one of the larger trees, because honeybees were swarming in and out of a hole in the trunk at eye level.

The sun was setting—high time the dog and I left for home.

*   *   *

For a purebred black Labrador, April turned out to be smaller than normal at maturity, even for a female. In the field, her natural hunting instincts were a pleasure to watch. With experience and guidance, I knew she would become a fine hunting companion, especially for waterfowl. But there would be plenty of time to train her for that. Obedience training came first.

Whether you live in a city or its suburbs, regardless of how docile the pet might be, local laws and ordinances prescribe control of your dog. And of course dogless neighbors are not all that fond of other people's pets.

In June, we started April on a once-a-week obedience training course with professional handlers. The variety of dogs entered in the class astounded me: German shepherd, dalmatian, collie, Pekingese, poodle, weimaraner, Irish setter, various spaniels, malemute, terrier, and who-knows-what-all.

April learned fast with choke-chain training. After we returned from the second session, I took the dog outside for a short romp in the yard at dusk. She never tired of running after a tennis ball and returning it to my feet. That night I thought she had tallied enough exercise for the day, so we went out the side door and I gave the wet ball a short toss into the front yard. April bounded after it, as she had done hundreds of times, and brought it back to me. When she came close enough, I reached down to take the ball from her mouth.

Without any warning, she fell on her right side with a plop, and the ball rolled away. The poor dog's tongue hung out, and she began the most pitiful moaning—as if in great pain. I instantly thought of poison again, but we had just returned from training class, where we knew she had eaten nothing. And she hadn't been outside until now.

I rubbed her chest and stomach briefly before dashing inside to call the vet. Gail ran out to April. The veterinarian said to bring the dog in as quickly as possible. Thoughts raced across my mind—she had received all necessary shots. I hurried out and tried to give her an antidote just in case. She had stopped kicking. I couldn't feel any pulse or detect any breathing, and her eyes were glazed. Gail and I stared blankly at each other, and couldn't—or didn't want to believe—our friendly pup was dead.

Why would a young dog die so suddenly? We had the body examined by specialists at the University of Minnesota the next day. They made an inconclusive report that our Lab "may have died from a heart attack." There was no sign of any disease.

Her name signified the entrance of spring—April, a time when birds return to cheer us up, and wildflowers perform their annual miracle—a time for blossoms and a blooming of the spirit, when the glowing change of season warms us with sunny optimism. That is when the puppy came into our lives, naive and eager to please, bumbling along on clumsy feet, with a whole new world to explore.

Born on Valentine's Day (appropriate, we thought, for all the love she shared with us), April left us just sixteen months later.

18 Honeybees—and Hornets

How doth the little busy bee
Improve each shining hour,
And gather honey all the day
From every opening flower!
Isaac Watts

Like other fanciers of honey, I had on occasion cut down a "bee tree" for the sweet reward. Now, in my first attempt at beekeeping, I was determined to set up a controlled hive. Observing their activities firsthand might salve my curiosity. Honeybees are a fascinating hobby, unless you are allergic to bee stings.

The hive should face southeast, the books said, to allow the bees maximum benefit of sunshine for each working day. I chose the south edge of the point of trees leading toward the round pond. There a veteran hard maple enjoyed full sunlight, and the hive could not be seen from our path. The bees should appreciate the big maple's crown of blossoms until wildflowers and clover came into bloom again. Also, their range of two miles from the hive would take in surrounding hayfields. Honeybees dearly love alfalfa blossoms, and the bloom furnishes tasty honey. Unknowingly, honeybees do alfalfa the favor of cross-pollination.

After I carried the standard-size hive boxes over, the bees were next. My two-pound "package" (approximately ten thousand honeybees, with one queen) had come through the mail from the deep South. They were enclosed in a screened container, and a can of sugar water dripped sustenance during transit. The queen travels separately in a tiny screen-covered box attached to the mass of bees. She usually has two or three attendants to share her space.

It is a trifle frightening the first time you release a colony of honeybees into a new hive. The boys watched warily from twenty feet away. I wore a protective veil and special elbow-length gloves,

163

but they weren't necessary. The long-bodied queen looked lively, and the worker bees immediately began serving her majesty. Now if the local bears would kindly leave the hive alone, we might have honey by fall.

After two months went by, the beehive was teaming with activity. Honeybees were hauling in dark pollen, and the brood had multiplied. With a wide choice of blossoms now available, the honey flow was in progress.

For the very first time, I removed a frame from the hive and took it over to camp. Golden honey dripped from the comb as I set it down on the table. We all slurped samples. With this initial reward, I felt accepted into the centuries-old occupation of beekeeping.

The hive frame included brood bees imprisoned in their wax "wombs." We studied the perfectly formed comb cells, and became absorbed in this marvel of nature. It has been proven that no other shape permits as many cells in a given space as does the interlocked pattern of hexagons. So exactly alike are these wax cells that they were once considered as a basis for an international unit of measurement.

Each worker bee secretes wax, which accumulates on its legs. Then, bit by bit, the bee chews off this wax to form the hexagonal cells.

Part of the timeless cycle of a honeybee colony unfolded before us—a young bee chose that moment for her "coming-out party." (I say "her" because all worker bees are females.) From inside, one antenna, then the other, cut through the wax cell cap. In almost imperceptible wiggly cutting movements, she sawed around the cell lid like a miniature can opener. The cell cap came off to expose the newborn bee's head, and she took her first peek at the world.

Each young bee is a snug fit inside the cell by the time she matures, and this one squirmed with obvious effort before struggling free. Both wings immediately spread out to dry while the young bee's legs stretched and flexed. Briefly, she staggered over the combs until she found a cell of honey to feed on before starting her first job of cleaning cells. In normal sequence, she'd next become a nurse bee for the larvae, helping to keep them warm. And she would also aid other worker bees in tending the queen, and later graduate to comb building. After about two weeks the new bee is ready to take on the duties of gathering pollen and nectar for the colony.

Worker bees are much smaller than drones (male bees, which have no stinger.) The drones do nothing to help the hive; their only purpose is to assure fertilization of a new queen when that becomes necessary. Out of hundreds of available drones, only eight or ten may mate with a new queen. Mating takes place in flight, and then the drones die. The fertilized queen can produce eggs—both male and female—for up to four seasons. When the honey flow ends each year, all drones are expelled from the hive to starve.

In September, I went straight to the beehive—for a disappointing shock. Something, or somebody, had knocked over the stack of hive boxes, exposing frames of honeycomb and brood cells. Bees clustered around the overturned hive, humming in confusion. It could not have been a bear or a badger (both are fond of bee larvae) because none of the comb frames were damaged. I had a suspect in mind; he probably pushed over the hives and ran, just to see if he could get away without being stung. Tomorrow I'd remove the bees, with whatever honey there might be, and take the hive home.

On Sunday morning, a light frost covered the ground. Good. Now the honeybees ought to be numb from the cold and less belligerent. I donned my beekeeper's veil and carried the hive boxes out to the garden near the road. Returning bees buzzed around the rock pile where the hive had been. No hive. No queen. Anyhow, I rationalized, worker bees live only about six weeks. (They literally work themselves to death.) It is a gamble trying to carry a colony through the winter, and more costly than starting over each year with a new package. Over fifty pounds of honey would be needed for enough bees to last until spring.

Three bees managed to get revenge by penetrating my armor. They all died heroines—especially the one that sneaked into my armpit to set her stinger!

There was very little honey to harvest that first year. I blamed the poor results on the culprit who shoved over the stacked hive. The queen, I suspected, had succumbed because of the vandal's senseless prank. To back up my theory, several new queen cells appeared in various stages of development. Normally, this does not take place if

165

the original queen remains healthy.

The following summer, in the heat of July, Nathan and I loaded the pickup for a visit to our woodland retreat. We threw in a dilapidated box spring; I planned to get rid of bulky odds and ends at the sanitary landfill near Larsville.

I wonder who invented the cover-up title of "sanitary landfill" to glorify a dump? Well, no matter what they chose to call it, it was closed when we got there. We'd have to dispose of our castoffs elsewhere.

After the usual stops in Larsville, we tried fishing on Tomahawk Lake below the dam. I filleted three keeper-size bass on the truck tailgate, and put them on ice. We'd have a meal of fresh fish in camp, and donate the raw leftovers to the mink and turtles.

On these northerly excursions, we often commented, "No two trips to the 80 are ever the same." And this time, a surprise awaited us.

The weeds were three feet high in our pulloff road. I backed the pickup in and took out the scythe to cut a swath toward camp. Nathan headed for the shack.

While I swung the scythe, working up a sweat, pesky deer flies dive bombed my head. Before I cleared ten feet of weeds, young Nathan let out a yell: "Dad! A bee stung me!"

He sounded on the verge of crying. I went around to the front of the shack to console him.

"Just deer flies," I said, "not as bad as a bee sting."

He didn't agree, but stood back while I leveled the small clearing in front of the shack.

"Is everything OK inside?" I asked as I set the scythe down.

"Haven't been in there yet," he answered glumly.

I unhooked the door and stepped inside. Nothing looked any— OW! The first one zapped me on the cheek in an instant. Then another, and another. Mad hornets swarmed at my head and arms. A few stung the top of my head. Hair did not stop them. A speedy glance at the ceiling revealed part of their gray celled nest. I swatted wildly and charged out the door to escape. Nathan ran to join me in thick bushes away from the shack. The hornets didn't follow us into the heavy cover.

"See, Dad! I *told* you they're bees!"

I could no longer argue the point. Hornets, wasps—whatever you called them, their stingers packed a lot more wallop than mosquitoes'. My head and arms burned all over; then the itching started.

Instead of driving to the nearest drugstore to get some kind of ointment, we went straight to Mother Nature. Near the ponds, jewel weed grows profusely in wet ground. (The tiny orange blossoms resemble a snapdragon's.) I yanked up a handful of the watery weeds and we sat down to treat ourselves. By breaking up the translucent stems and swabbing the juice over our puffy welts, we soothed the itching. Even if the herbal medicine fell short of a pharmacist's prescription, it afforded us prompt relief, free of charge.

For the time being, those winged devils were in complete command of the shack. Driving seventeen miles to town for a sleeping room didn't make sense, even though we had no tent along. We did have the pickup and, by rare circumstance, the old box spring to sleep on. Made to order. Although the truck's camper lacked a rear wall, at least we'd have a roof over our heads for the night.

It took us a while to rearrange junk and gear in the back of the pickup. I fastened mosquito netting across the open end of the truckbed and threw a section of discarded carpet onto the roof; anchored by rocks, it could be draped over the netting at bedtime.

After sundown, we built a comforting campfire in the roadbed behind the truck. With the shack off limits, the cooking utensils were out of reach, and so were our plans for frying fish. Food we had aplenty, but how do you broil a hamburger over a fire without any frying pan or grill? Even the aluminum foil was in the shack beyond our grasp.

I rummaged through the truck and came up with a quart pan, generally used only for boiling vegetables. Today it would have to serve a different purpose, although I could only cook one burger at a time.

In due course, Nathan beamed, "Tastes great!"

I made a belated apology to him for misinterpreting his warning about the wasps. He quickly forgave me, and allowed as how I got the worst end of the deal anyway.

After dark, we piled wood on the campfire and retreated into the

167

truck camper. Secure behind the mosquito netting, we gazed into the blaze, and I told Nathan about some of my past experiences with hornets.

Yellow jackets, hornets—anything in the wasp family has a mean disposition. They are most irritable insects when disturbed. As a hobby beekeeper, I can tell you I would much rather be stung by a honeybee than a wasp. For one thing, a worker bee can sting only once, and then she dies, whereas a wasp can zap you again and again. Furthermore, I learned the hard way that disturbed yellow jackets will *follow* you to carry out their vengeance.

It happened when my son Alan and I were float fishing on the Mississippi. We ran out of bait, and pulled up on an island to dig some worms. Alan found a pile of driftwood and boards in the weeds, and he lifted up a piece to look for earthworms. He yelled, "Hornets!" and raced past me. A sharp stab on the cheek sent me flying after him. We stopped about twenty yards away to collect our wits, and immediately got stung two or three more times. That did it! We made a speedy loop back to the boat and shoved off to safety.

Once when I was about four years old, I had a memorable encounter with the worrisome pests. We were playing behind the barn; my brother Charles, age six, made an idle suggestion: "Why don't you crawl under that old wagon over there and get that cabbage?"

I have a vague recollection of suspicion; somehow it didn't jibe, that a cabbage would grow in a place like that. But when your older brother eggs you on, there is no way out. It *did* resemble a cabbage, and with my curiosity aroused, I squirmed under the wagon and made a grab for it. Ow-eee! I swung and swatted at mad hornets and ran bawling to the trout stream that flowed through our pasture. Charles, secured by distance, rolled in the grass and laughed himself silly.

The cold water had a pacifying effect, temporarily. My face and arms soon puffed up from hornet stings. Our mother heard the commotion, and big brother stopped laughing. When she found out what happened—loudly verified by the victim—Charles got the seat of his pants warmed up. Only years later could we both laugh at the episode.

Last fall, while I had been painting shelf boards outside the shack, I swatted one persistent wasp with the wet paint brush. A partial coat of robin's egg blue put an end to his annoying distraction.

In late summer, yellow jackets tend to fan out over wider territory. Any fresh odor or peculiar scent attracts them—uncovered refuse, beverage containers (especially if sweet liquid)—and in this case, paint.

Inside the shack that day, a lone wasp buzzed around, upsetting my peaceful pursuits. I followed the yellow jacket to the shack's window, seeking long delayed revenge for past transgressions of his kind. When he buzzed against the glass near a spider web in one corner, I saw my chance. With the swing of a towel, he was swept into the web.

The wasp struggled in vain. His vibrations brought a spider out to greet the catch. She used caution—not too close at first. Then she tacked a sticky strand to one of the wasp's legs. And another. His body arched and twisted, and his stinger came out, but the spider stayed out of reach. She appeared to test the victim by sparring at him with two widely spread front legs.

While the mother spider was securing the wasp, a young spider moved in to help. He threw a web or two onto a twitching leg while she worked. Abruptly she chased him off. This was *her* dinner.

Presently, mama spider edged up and bit the wasp behind its head, and he stopped moving.

When I checked a few minutes later, the spider was drawing fluid from the body of the wasp. After a few hours, the insect had shrunk to a hollow shell. And still later, his remains hung in a neatly wrapped ball of webbing.

The stories . . . staring into the campfire . . . Nathan and I were ready for a good night's sleep in the truck. We felt like pioneers after overcoming an obstacle on the trail: "The oxen are fed, and the covered wagons gathered in a circle. Now if the Indians don't attack at dawn . . ."

Nathan logged sleep through the quiet night. Oh, to be his age again!

Long before daylight, I heard a distant rumbling in the west. Thunder rolled closer until I saw flashes of lightning through a small opening above the tailgate. The storm moved steadily toward us.

169

More lightning, with a crash of thunder, jolted Nathan awake at dawn. We both sat up to consider our safety.

"What if it strikes the truck?" he wanted to know.

"Vehicles are generally safe shelters from lightning," I assured him, "because they rest on rubber tires."

Another thunderous crash, and I hoped my theory held together. The trees on either side of us didn't pose much threat—they were medium-size aspen and oaks.

The rain increased to a heavy downpour. In our dry truck shelter, we fully enjoyed the sound of rain splattering on the tinny roof. A half hour later, the storm moved on, and we climbed out of the truck to stretch.

Our campfire had become a soggy mass of ashes and blackened stubs of wood. I cleaned it out and reached under the truck for some dry sticks I had stashed there the night before. We heated water in our only utensil, the all-purpose pan, for instant coffee and hot chocolate with rolls.

Barely did we finish breakfast before the rains came again. Back into the camper shelter. In between showers, we hauled the box spring out of the truck and dropped it in a clearing behind the shack. It had served its purpose. The dump was too far away—might as well burn it safely now in wet weather.

I poured gasoline over the fabric, left a lighting trail as a fuse, and took the can back to the truck. With Nathan a safe distance away, I lit the fuel end in the grass. Flames leaped along the line, and *pfoof*, the box spring was ablaze.

Another shower chased us into the truck, and we agreed to give it up. Next time, I'd come prepared to engage those hornets in chemical warfare, and regain control of the shack.

19 Grampa and Bears

But now I am . . . cribbed, confined, bound in to saucy
doubts and fears.
William Shakespeare

Only traces of snow remained late in April, and the ponds were at full capacity. In the brown slough, marsh marigolds presented the first green of spring, blossoming gold.

This time my father came along to shake the winter doldrums. A retired farmer couldn't resist the chance to turn over some soil; at home, Grampa still tended a big garden at the age of 83.

He and I transplanted three tamaracks and a Norway spruce, and then set out a lilac and honeysuckle bush to add variety. The apple and plum trees showed signs of budding.

A few songbirds were back from the South, and the main thrust of birds would be returning soon. The perennial pair of phoebes had already built a nest under a corner of the shack's roof; it held one tiny white egg. The male always arrives a few days ahead of his mate. No one can explain why, although phoebes pair for life, they do not travel north together.

Several mallards cruised the ponds, and a noisy pair of courting wood ducks splashed in the water. Raccoons had been patrolling the muddy beaver dam in search of emerging frogs. Alan opened the dam and water rushed across the high ground between ponds. There is something fascinating about fast-flowing water, and a day's drainage would never be missed by the beavers in springtime.

Grampa and I strolled down the gravel road to see how close the backed-up water came to overflowing the right-of-way. Since last year's county crew had raised the road level, just a trickle crossed there. A few yards past the low spot, we examined a wet streak across the road. Full-size bear tracks told the tale. At this point, a bear had sloshed out of the marsh from the east side, crossed the road, and plowed his way west into our waters and woods.

"Stones o' Thor!" Grampa exclaimed.

I had no idea where he got that expression, but I knew by now that it showed consternation.

"He sure picked the hard way," Grampa commented.

"Yeah—all he had to do was follow the beaver dam for easy walking," I agreed.

And yet, the bear probably had a purpose. We surmised that he was hungry after hibernation, and wallowed through the water eating cattail tubers and other succulent roots. If he could catch an unwary muskrat or beaver on the way, so much the better for his diet.

This discovery kept Grampa near camp. *He feared bears.* They are not to be trusted, he maintained. And to back up his claim, he reminded me of what took place about fifty miles north of our woods a few years earlier.

A lone trout fisherman failed to return from a remote stream, and a party of searchers went looking for him the next day. Eventually they came upon shreds of clothing and a flyrod. The searchers followed a trail of blood to the man's mangled body in the brush. They could only speculate on what took place: perhaps, without realizing it, the hapless fisherman came between a sow and her cub.

Although cases of black bears attacking humans are rare, there are exceptions to the rule. Any wild animal is subject to moods, good and bad. An older bear could be grumpy from bad teeth or other aches and pains that come with age.

At the time, my only encounter with a black bear in the woods had been almost comical. Inland from Lake Superior on a summer day, I went out to dig worms near a backwoods garbage dump. (Sometimes at night, after a hard day's fishing, we drove over there to watch bears scrounge for food. In the safety of a car, we could watch them in our headlights.) But in daylight, I didn't expect to see any bears around. Armed only with a spade and a pail, I rounded the bend of a well-used bear trail. Just then a big bear came up over a bank to my right, thirty feet away. My first thought was "it can't be." My

174

second thought—"I wish I could fly." For an instant we each froze in a what-are-*you*-doing-here stance. In a flash we both wheeled to retreat in opposite directions. In this case, it was just something to laugh at with my fishing buddies. Grampa, however, failed to find any humor in my story.

Back at the car, we unloaded a better box spring for the bunkbed. Mice had been using one of the mattresses as a rich source of nesting material. Under the ceiling rafter at the back, I grabbed a handful of soft fibers, and a mouse scurried away. There was another nest inside the pocket of an old coat hanging on the wall.

Grampa had never seen beavers in natural habitat. He crouched in the weeds and stared at each one with all the intensity of a cat stalking a bird.

One of April's misty drizzles moved through, and by dark a heavy cloud bank rolled in from the southwest. It felt good to be warm and dry inside the shack that night.

On Monday morning, a crew of workmen unloaded a shiny galvanized culvert on the road close to where the bear had crossed. Cars seldom used this road on weekdays. If one came by while they were replacing the culvert, it must either wait or go back north four miles to the blacktop highway.

The men spent half a day trenching in the new culvert. Just as they finished, a car came down the road from the north. The driver's timing couldn't have been better.

* * *

Grampa joined me again in the fall, and we visited the Frenchman in his trailer house on the edge of Larsville. Fabre, not being aware of my dad's aversion to bears, had a new story.

"Bears been killing sheep down the road from your shack. And behind Crazy's place, I hear a guy shot two bears a coupla' weeks ago. He put out bait—a goat carcass, dead fish, and stuff—and built a tree stand to wait for 'em. Five bears came by, and he got two of 'em."

That sounded close to the shack, Grampa knew, but he withheld comment. No bear would come around while we were hammering on siding.

At the lumber yard, we tied ten sheets of 4 x 8 chipboard atop the station wagon.

As soon as we unloaded the siding in camp, Grampa went over to look for beavers. For him, those "odd little critters" were the main attraction up here—and not as dangerous as bears. Grampa dubbed our woods "the wild 80"—hence the title for this book.

I finished the west side of the shack with chipboard, and it gave the building a dressed-up look. Without electricity for a power tool, it went slow, hand-sawing the 4 x 8 panels to fit the roof angle. The power line was only forty yards away, but with no hookup, it might as well have been forty miles. I'd have to do it the hard way, as my carpenter grandfather (Grampa's dad) did. Although I never knew my grandfather, I inherited his tools—if not his skills in carpentry. Some of the houses and barns he built in the 1890s are still shipshape. In thirty years (optimistically) this shack might be obliterated, but for now it remained our haven from the elements.

Although porous popple burns up fast, the supply was endless. Black tar dripped from the hillbilly chimney outside, and I could see why they don't advise using aspen logs in a fireplace. Up here it didn't matter—cheap heat, if you discounted the labor.

Grampa and I grilled steaks over coals. When they came to a crusty brown, we sat down for a feast in the warm sun.

The Frenchman came by and took us over to Lindstroms' cabin in his pickup. Deer season would open tomorrow, and some of the hunters were already there.

Oscar showed us the damage done to their cabin sometime during the previous year. At first glance, I thought vandals had shotgunned off the front corner of the cabin's roof—both corners, in fact.

"No-o . . . it was the *bear*," Oscar emphasized. "He *bit off all four corners* of the roof!"

Grampa gulped.

The Lindstrom cabin was three times the size of our shack, with the same style of sloping flat roof. The bear had left his mark in the boards of each corner overhang—unmistakable teeth imprints and raking claw grooves down from the top.

"He's a big brute," Oscar continued. "Look at this." And he led us

176

around to the rear. The cabin roof stood about seven feet high back there. At his suggestion, I climbed up on a homemade ladder to examine the damage.

"That's no small bear. You can see he stood on his hind legs' and reached over the top to claw the roof. This ladder wasn't here when *he* came by," Oscar added with a chuckle.

The Frenchman told us he had seen a bear the year before, crossing the road near Lindstroms' frontage. "Good-sized bear," he assured us. "Might've been this one."

"He's been here three times now," Oscar said. "First time, he broke in before we had the cabin finished. That's when he shredded up the sleeping bag. Next time he did this. And the last time, he knocked over the outhouse over there and chewed up the roof on it."

Lucky nobody was in it, we all laughed. Grampa said little, but I knew what he was thinking—"Stones o' Thor!"

For some reason, the bear held a grudge against that cabin. To be sure, it represented an encroachment on his hunting territory. But more than that, he may have resented the intrusion of "progress." The bear was accustomed to roaming a wide area, and this man-made structure cropped up in his path to challenge his reclusive routine. Things just weren't *natural* anymore. Not unlike human vandals, he vented his wrath in destruction.

The Frenchman dropped us off at the shack, and I still wondered about the bear. Why hadn't the beast bothered our humble abode? Maybe he did not feel safe near a road.

Since then, Oscar and his wife have seen the bear. "We happened along one day in time to watch him cross the road near our driveway . . . *huge bear!*" Oscar claims. "We got within thirty yards of him, in the pickup, and you could see his muscles rippling under shiny black fur. That bear was in no hurry; he even stopped in the road to stare at the truck . . . acted like he owned the place. Shoulda' had a camera."

After they were certain the bear had moved on, Oscar got out to look at tracks in the mud. "His pawprint measured eight inches; now that's a *big bear,*" he exclaimed. "Prob'ly an old boar. A game warden I know has live-trapped 'problem' bears for transport, and he's never seen one with a footprint that size. His guess is this one weighs at least five hundred pounds. Must be the one that's always chompin' up my cabin."

We picked up around camp. I took a short hike in the woods before we left, and Grampa chose to guard the shack, because walking along the beaver dam was too difficult with a cane. (Besides, who knows what might be lurking in the dark woods?)

We loaded the car, and I turned the key in the ignition. *Click.* Nothing more. The battery was down. Passing cars were few and far between on this road. I'd have to walk to the closest farm to seek help.

At least it was the middle of a sunny day; Grampa took a fresh pinch of Copenhagen and said he would wait in the car. (Bears, you know.)

I kicked rocks for a mile or so on the gravel road till I reached Clarence's farm.

"Gee, all the men are gone," his wife told me after I explained my predicament. "But you might find Floyd home, across the road. He's retired."

Floyd's wife came to the door, and she didn't look like the mechanic type either. I began to wonder how many miles I'd have to hoof it before finding aid. Then Floyd appeared, and I made my plea for his services. In a few minutes we were back at the shack.

Grampa dozed in the car, with the windows up, probably dreaming about bears. He didn't hear our approach. When the two bumpers met, his head popped up and he almost swallowed his snoose!

I hooked up the jumper cables to each battery, and Floyd revved up his motor. On the second try, the motor turned over.

I asked Floyd what we owed him for the inconvenience, and without hesitation he replied, "I'd like to hunt deer in your woods."

That caught me by surprise. I had never seen him before this day, and had no idea he coveted these woods for hunting. What could I say? Hunting with strangers is against my principles (self-preservation), but he appeared to be in his late sixties, mentally and physically sound.

That is more than I could say for two young men who pulled up in front of the 80 one fall. They asked for permission to hunt deer with bow and arrow. One of the pair was really flying—hopped up on some unnamed adulteration. Even clear-headed hunters have a low success ratio in archery. I wouldn't want to be within ten miles of such "hunters" as those two clunks imagined themselves to be.

The prolific bruins are expanding their territory. Just last fall more than forty black bears were taken in our county, where farmers report the occasional loss of a calf or sheep. Because most kills take place at night, the act is rarely witnessed. With some domestic animal kills, coyotes may deserve the blame heaped on bears. Still, a full-grown cow or a horse will sometimes fall victim to a bear.

Not far from the wild 80, one farmer shot five bears he caught in the act of demolishing his cornfield. The season limit is one animal per hunter, but by law a farmer is allowed to protect his crops.

An incident in September 1987 underlines Grampa's long-held distrust of black hears. Two campers were mauled by a rogue bear in the Boundary Waters Canoe Area wilderness of northern Minnesota in unprovoked attacks. On Monday a teenage college student from Tennessee suffered bites, scratches, and a fractured shoulder blade. The bear charged him on the shore of Lady Boot Bay and gave chase into the shallow water. The young man's screams for help brought friends from nearby, but they were in a canoe and unarmed. The two canoers jumped out and whacked at the bear with the only weapon at hand, canoe paddles. The animal released its hold on the youth long enough for him to be hustled into the canoe and paddled out of reach. Next day, the victim was flown to a hospital in Ely, Minnesota for treatment.

On that day, less than twenty-four hours later and only a mile from the first attack, another camper was mauled by a bear. This time a middle-aged man and his son were breaking camp, carrying packs to their canoe on Wabang Lake. Without a sound, the black bear came out of the woods toward the men. They yelled and waved their arms to scare off the bear, but he kept coming and charged the older man, who ran and dove into shallow water. The bear was soon on top of him, biting him on the back of his neck and clawing at his shoulders, arms, and thigh. Again, a canoe paddle was all his son had to drive off the bear. As the two men hurriedly shoved off in their canoe, the bear plowed into the water after them. They quickly found help from nearby campers and were relayed by boat and plane to a hospital in Cook. The son got off without a scratch, and he probably saved his father's life.

Department of Natural Resources conservation officers immediately put out bait in the vicinity and then shot a small female bear they believed responsible for both attacks. The animal's carcass was flown to the University of Minnesota's St. Paul campus, Department of Veterinary Diagnostic Investigation. Examiners determined that the bear did not have rabies—nor did they find evidence of brain tumors, old wounds, broken teeth, or any overload of parasites. The bear was undernourished, and weighed only 117 pounds. (Much less than either attack victim had guessed!)

Proof that the right bear had been killed came from diagnosis of human hairs found in its stomach and compared to both men involved. Exhaustive tests were made by the state health department, DNR bear biologists, and the crime laboratory of the State Bureau of Criminal Apprehension in St. Paul.

Why did this particular bear attack humans? According to Lynn Rogers of Ely, MN., a world-renowned expert on black bears: "We may never know. Black bears usually avoid people, but in this case none of the tests offered a solution to the attack. It might have been a mental or other health problem. Like people, animals have different personalities, and this one was out of step with her kind."

And Rogers adds, "Unprovoked, predatory attacks by black bears are rare, but they get big press coverage. These two rogue bear attacks in the BWCA are the first I've ever heard of in that area, even with 100,000 visitors each year. Although noncaptive black bears have accounted for 23 deaths in North America since 1900, by comparison, a person is about 180 times more likely to be killed by a bee sting than by a black bear."

Even so, it's best to treat a bear (or any wild animal) as potentially dangerous—or at very least, unpredictable.

Shortly after the much publicized bear/human scuffles in the Boundary Waters country, I stopped by to visit Riley. He lives on a back road not far from my woods, and he keeps me posted on local events concerning both people and wildlife. While we chatted, I asked if he had seen any bears lately. Riley took a deep breath, and with a twinkle in his eye, told this tale.

"One night last month [September] at about two in the morning, our dogs were howlin' such a racket I couldn't sleep, so I got up to see if they'd treed a 'coon. Leaves were still on the trees, and my flashlight picked up a patch of fur way up in that elm by the house. Well, I had my .22 pistol so I took a pop at the 'coon and he let out a loud 'AW-W-RRR' like no coon I ever heard! Gave me a chill, I'll tellya—I hollered to the missus, 'It's a bear!' and to stay in the house and keep the back door open. Took another shot and he roared ag'in, then came a-crashin' down through the limbs—landed right at my feet. I quick emptied the pistol into him and he quit growlin'; there was another bear over by the sheep, and he took off. The dogs all went quiet, and none of 'em felt like givin' chase," he grinned.

Riley said the dead bear "went about 250 pounds . . . had a nice shiny coat." He didn't want the bear's skull, so I kept it as a souvenir.

The following winter was a time of sadness. Grampa passed away suddenly from a heart attack. A death in the family sets aside trivial complaints of everyday living, and something in the human psyche pushes memories of good things to the surface. It helps us to carry on with images of pleasures shared, music and laughter. Reminiscing. My dad worked hard all his life, and he spent most of his years in fine health. How he enjoyed hunting in the hills of southeastern Minnesota; neither he nor I ever missed a season down there. Successful or not, we teamed up for the joys of roving those wooded hills.

Grampa did not spend his last days in a hospital bed. He died quickly, out-of-doors, under the sky, while walking down a country road.

20 Adventure and Adversity

Prosperity doth best discover vice, but adversity doth best discover virtue.
Francis Bacon

Life can't be all sweetness and light—not when you're roughing it in the hinterland. There are days when—

On a mild January weekend before the shack was built, the boys and I couldn't resist a one-day trip to the winter woods. The ponds were at rest under a thick layer of white, and the boys worked feverishly to chop a hole in the ice. They just *had* to find out how thick it might be. I have never felt safe on ice over deep water, and I cautioned them to avoid the area of nine-foot depth.

The beaver lodge resembled an Eskimo igloo, with an organized jumble of sticks jutting from its roof of snow. I crossed the frozen pond, and a few feet short of the lodge, I suddenly dropped through thin ice into cold water, knee deep; another yard to the right and I would have gone in over my head. I had blundered onto the beavers' entrance lane, where ice stayed thinner.

I scrambled out over the lodge and hurried to our camp clearing. It seemed like forever before we got a bonfire going. My wet pants legs froze stiff as a board in their crinkled form. Since I had no extra boots or dry socks along, there was nothing to do but prop my purple feet near the fire to thaw. Jack London's "To Build A Fire" came to mind.

The following spring, we strolled into our clearing to check the salt lick for tracks, and found a neatly clipped row of deer hair. A poacher? The hair was cut off cleanly on the ends, as if by a bullet or an arrow. There was no sign of a carcass—probably a near miss. I decided to move the salt block farther back in the woods.

183

That afternoon, I was busy planting while the boys were fooling around the ponds. Abruptly, shouts came from across the road. Black smoke billowed over the treetops. *A fire on the farm!* I ran out to the road, spade in hand—quickly joined by Tommy, Alan, and Nathan.

The farm's machine shed was ablaze, and fire had already spread to the hayfield stubble. Two young men were beating at the fire's leading edge where it was eating its way toward the hermit's woods. The farm shed was doomed. Flames rapidly consumed its dry wall boards, and the roof fell in with a muffled *whoosh*.

We did our best to contain the fire in the hayfield by stomping and spading, but the ground was very dry, and flames licked into the brush. A light wind was blowing away from the house and barn; at least those buildings looked safe.

Grass burning in the ditch worried me most. If sparks blew across the road into marsh grass on our side, we'd lose the battle.

But the wind held true, and the accidental arsonists at last succeeded in containing the fire just inside the edge of the woods. We all spread out to keep a wary eye on the smoking brush until it came to a smoldering standstill. The shed was the only real loss, because the charred hayfield would soon turn green again at this time of year.

Neither of the fellows who started the fire felt very talkative. They hadn't asked for our help, and they didn't bother to thank us for it. One of them was the new owner's son, and he planned to move onto the farm before long. Covered with soot and smelling of acrid smoke, the boys and I returned to camp.

This trip was the first for my youngest son, Nathan, joining the "big boys" away from his mother's apron strings, and how the five-year-old loved it. That evening, while I shared the campfire with him, Nathan confided: "Y'know, Dad . . . Mom gets so boring up here, but we got *all* the fun!" We grinned at each other in the warm glow of the firelight.

On a warm night in July, we were all in the tent (not visible from the road) when we heard a car pull up and stop. Our car was parked out there. Visitors, after dark? Seldom did anyone stop to see us here, even in daylight. Vandals? Thieves? We held our collective breath and listened. No voices. We had no light on to pinpoint our location in the trees.

"Maybe it's just the game warden looking for poachers?" I suggested.

"Or robbers!" one of the boys whispered. "Where's the rifle?"

We could hear a car motor running, but no talking. Shortly, they drove away, leaving us guessing; would they return later that night? It took us awhile to settle down to sleep.

And on another summer night when we were still in the tent stage, it was abnormally quiet. Even the frogs were resting. Both tired boys were logging sleep for tomorrow's adventures. A solitary mosquito droned aloft inside the dark canvas, plotting its chance to draw blood. I slapped blindly and missed, gave up and dozed off . . .

A few hours later, I awoke to the sound of a car—a rarity on this isolated road, especially late at night. It turned into the farmyard driveway across the road, a quarter of a mile from our hideaway. All went quiet again—briefly. Murmuring voices escalated to a crescendo of soprano shrieks. The high voltage of female accusations charged the air, and the shrill wail of a wronged woman scratched the stillness. I overheard enough in the distance to gather that the young man's wife suspected him of a gross breach of marital contract. It took me awhile to get back to sleep, but the boys heard nothing at all.

The next day, after a long hike in the woods, we were returning to camp. Nathan ran ahead of me, and Alan had stopped at the beaver lodge. Dogs began barking nearby; I hurried toward camp.

Two snarling stray dogs stood their ground in front of Nathan, barking and baring their fangs in defiance. The surly mongrels had made a shambles of our campground, scattering eggshells, empty cans, and refuse all around. I lifted the .22 rifle and fired a shot over their heads. Only then did the marauders turn tail, barking as they ran.

In man or beast, self-preservation is a most powerful instinct. Crazed by starvation, the vicious dogs might well have attacked the small boy if I hadn't come along. The incident left me slightly shaken as we cleaned up the mess.

On one visit to the woods—Good Friday, or so the calendar read—I parked in the pulloff road. The first thing I noticed was a flat tire. At least we had made it to our destination; there would be no cars whizzing by in this peaceful setting.

In the process of trying to remove the wheel, I broke off two lugbolts. After some experimenting, I discovered that this make of car had *reverse threads,* but only on the left side. The nuts there had to be turned *clockwise* to get the wheel off. Crazy engineering!

With the spare tire on, I heaved a sigh of relief. Prematurely, as it turned out.

The surface frost was gone, and the ground tested firm underfoot. However, the narrow driveway made a sharp jog left to our clearing, and that was my undoing—the car bogged down.

For the next two hours, Nathan and I shoveled mud out from under all four wheels, carried gravel from the road, tried putting boards beneath the tires—nothing worked, it only got worse. The car now rested on its underside, and the rear wheels were down to frostline, spinning on ice. Sweaty and disgusted, we admitted defeat and went out to the road to "wish" for help from a passing car. Nobody on this road today.

We carried paraphernalia in to the shack, always listening carefully for the sound of an approaching car.

Hours later, I hailed two men in a pickup truck. We hooked up the tow chain, but their tires were too bald to grip the wet topsoil; they just spun deeper. It soon became evident that their vehicle would be stuck, too.

They did not leave us stranded. One man stayed while the other drove us to the nearest farm. By this time it was the supper hour, and I hated to impose.

"No, we just finished," the men assured me. One of them left the table and followed us back in his pickup.

The four-wheel drive made short work of it; our car jerked free, and I left it out by the road. Although my thanks flowed profusely, nobody would accept any payment.

I was struck by the contrasting attitude of people in rural versus urban settings. Up here in the woods, people were willing—almost anxious—to help a stranger in distress. On the other end of the scale of human kindness, I thought about a previous experience in the city. On our way home from work one day, a friend and I ran out of gas on a busy highway. We walked to a residential area, and knocked on the door of the first house we came to. A man answered, and we asked to buy a gallon of gasoline. He growled, *"Not now . . . I'm eatin',"* and slammed the door.

The primitive life isn't all milk and honey, but the good times afield far outweigh the days of adversity. Things looked brighter in the morning. Birds were singing, grouse drumming, and the sun came out; even the owls hooted happiness. A pair of pileated woodpeckers swept past, and near the shack, a brown snowshoe munched in contentment.

Spring drainage attracted Nathan to the north end of the island. He didn't mind mud at all—in an atmosphere of fun. Delighted with our temporary creek, he toiled to clean out the beaver-plugged culvert to speed up the current.

Along the ridge, each stack of firewood claimed a sheltered patch of snow. On the south end of the island, piles of four-foot logs were standing in shallow water. Loss of some wood there looked inevitable.

Nathan was engrossed in the enchantment of water flowage when I came by again. The thirty-inch culvert drew water to full capacity from the overflowing beaver dam above it. The boy left his watery paradise just long enough for a quick lunch before running back to the glorious stream. I opted for a short nap.

After that I emptied the shack of gear, and stuffed the car. Somehow, the equipment multiplied for every return trip.

Then I called for Nathan. No answer. I honked the car horn and waited; still no sign of him. An awful thought gave me a chill—what if he'd fallen into the water and the torrent had trapped him inside the culvert? Leaving him alone over there was unforgivable if—

With mounting apprehension, I hurried across the island, yelling his name louder and louder. My stomach tied itself in knots. When I had almost reached the culvert crossing, he came running around the bend with a frightened look on his face.

Immense relief charged through me, and yet I met him with an angry barrage (the disobeyed parent). "Didn't hear you" were his only words as he hurried past me toward the car.

Given my state of emotion at the time, I'm sure he saw me as some kind of ogre. We traveled awhile in uncommon silence before I broke the ice. I apologized for my tirade, and asked him if he knew why I had been so severe with him.

"Because you were afraid I might've drowned or somethin'," he answered softly.

I smiled inwardly, and put an arm around his shoulders. My youngest boy understood more than I had given him credit for; our conversation eased back to normal after that.

*　　*　　*

Only in late summer, while the water level was down, could I hope to accomplish anything with the galvanized culvert. It was submerged in three feet of water beside the deep pond, and had been useless to us for several years after the beavers came. Now we needed the culvert to improve our road across the island. Alone this time, I would wrestle with a long, unwieldy steel cable in an effort to prepare the culvert for being hauled out by machine.

I donned old denims, emptied all pockets, put on tennis shoes, and tucked the pants legs into my socks. Strong rubber bands held the cuffs snugly around my ankles to keep out bloodsuckers. With a spade in one hand and a garden hoe in the other, I waded waist deep into the pond.

My feet sank into soft, silted muck, and my pants legs bulged with pond water below the knees. By probing with the spade, I found the end of the culvert closest to shore, and proceeded to dig blindly underwater along one side. Each spadeful of mud and weeds churned up the water more. Perhaps hogs, buffalo, and elephants enjoy such wallowing, but I did not.

After digging under one side of the culvert for a length of four feet, I moved to the other side. One end had to hang free underneath or I could never get the cable around the culvert. While I slopped and sloshed, a curious duck swam around the bend ten feet away to see what on earth was taking place in her pond. At sight of the mad mud monster, she gave one frantic squawk and took flight.

After two hours of muckraking, I lifted the final rock obstacle from below one end of the culvert. The cable went on nicely with the first try; I walked carefully along the hidden, slippery top rings of the submerged culvert to loosen the other end.

As I returned to the bank, a black, writhing leech undulated its six-inch length across the surface. I scooped it up with the spade. When the leech dropped on soil, it contracted to short, fat size. On shore, I checked my pants legs to see if I had exposed any bare skin to the little bloodsuckers—I had visions of Humphrey Bogart wading the river in *The African Queen*.

Although native leeches are a popular bait for walleye fishermen, most people get the willies when they see one. Actually, a leech is quite harmless. In fact, it anesthetizes as it bites, and you'll never feel a thing. Furthermore, a leech injects an anticoagulant into the victim's bloodstream. And to top it off, the leech secretes a kind of antiseptic when it finishes feeding, so there is no danger of infection.

Only recently has the medical world discovered the benefits of using leeches to restore severed appendages. Since one species is even capable of dissolving blood clots, the future looks bright for the slithery little creature.

Clean water and dry clothes at the shack lifted my spirits, so I went over to the farmyard to see the welldigger in action. For three hours that morning while I worked on the culvert, his methodical rig had been hammering away. Hours on end of that rhythmic, monotonous pounding could put anyone to sleep, in spite of the noise.

"Having fun?" I greeted the man in between clanks.

"Not exactly," was his laconic reply.

His derricklike machine was mounted on the tail end of a flatbed trailer. A growing puddle of ochre clay ooze formed on the ground to one side of the shaft.

"I'm down about eighty feet, and still no water," he announced. At the rate of $10.50 per foot for drilling, (and that charge holds forth regardless of whether water is *ever* found) the absentee farm owner was running up a sizable bill.

The welldigger stopped his rig and the cable wound up rapidly to draw forth the pounding shaft. He dipped a pail of water from a barrel and poured it down the hole; then he lowered the steel pounding bar again for more hammering.

"Haven't hit any granite yet, anyhow," he commented. "That can be slow going when you have to drill."

I thought about the huge slabs of granite at the quarry a few miles to the west. Over there, the granite is near the surface, alongside a river.

"I've hit granite at 135 feet in parts of this county," the welldigger pointed out.

I looked down the gaping hole of the old well a few feet away. The cover boards were rotted, and the pump had fallen in, but it could be salvaged for the new well.

The welldigger shut off his motor and left for lunch in town. He climbed into the smaller truck, waved, and rattled down the farm driveway.

I turned toward camp, hoping we'd have a handy source of water again.

The shack roof required attention. Rain had dripped onto the top bunk mattress, and I could see light at one end of the ceiling. I used a stepladder to climb up the back side of the shack to check the roof.

The sun's heat had curled the edges of the roof roll, and there were cracks around some nailheads. As a temporary measure, I daubed on roofing tar.

When I tried to climb down off the overhanging roof, my feet missed the top of the short stepladder. Fortunately, I had a firm grip, because suddenly I found myself hanging there, legs dangling in space. Both arms felt as if they had stretched to gorilla length before I dropped to the ground.

In August, Alan and I loaded the old car with four hundred pounds of roofing shingles. Overloaded would be more correct—thirty-five miles out of town, we heard a *BANG* as loud as a cannon. The car's springs looked OK, so we continued north, but it was like riding a lumber wagon after that.

On the last mile of gravel road, there was a deep puddle in a low spot. A blue heron stood in the water, and it lifted off as our car dragged into view. As we drove through the wet depression, the muffler crunched off the car. From there on it was noisy driving, but we made it to the shack. Later, we found out the car's frame had cracked.

By the time we carried in the heavy shingles, Alan and I were ready for a campfire feast of corn on the cob, fresh garden tomatoes, and smoke-flavored hamburgers.

We nailed on the new roof next day, and took a back-road shortcut for home. At a familiar crossroad, the farmhouse was missing. Hollyhocks were in bloom around its foundation; the house must have burned down the previous winter.

A crew was at work widening one stretch of gravel road, and we barely coaxed the sagging old car through to solid roadbed. Just as we reached blacktop, the car overheated. I found a half-inch pebble lodged in the fanbelt wheel, and the belt was off. No tools. We mumbled and grumbled until a pickup came along. The man stopped, but said his tool kit was in a different vehicle. He poked around in his truck and finally found *one wrench*. Fat chance of that being the right size . . . but it fit perfectly!

With the fanbelt back in place, the old car got us home—slower, rougher, and louder than ever before. And that was its final trip.

After four years in the navy, nephew Tommy came back to the wild 80. The "kid" had about doubled his height since he first romped through these woods with me and my sons. Now his six feet, four inches, forced me to look up instead of down. How glad he was to be on familiar soil, in contrast to riding the high seas.

The duck season opened at noon. Mallards were plentiful, and we had good pass shooting on the island. A rubber raft came in handy for retrieving our duck dinners, but I waded into a beaver trench and took on a hip boot full of ice-cold water. At about that time, a trespasser began shooting on the mainland side of the island. I yelled at him, and at first he ignored me. The water between us foiled any closer confrontation, but I persisted until the brazen stranger moved off our land.

Tommy wanted to see how much those pine and spruce seedlings had grown during his absence. He was amazed. Some spruce were higher than his head, though our pine seedlings were long gone, succeeded by birch and aspen sprouts.

We happened onto a dead mallard; it was probably one shot that morning by the duck poacher. Payment received. It completed our possession limit for opening day.

Lyle, who lived on a farm down the road, came over the next morning for duck hunting. The three of us were about to leave camp

191

when two pickups slammed to a stop out on the road. Game wardens. They strode resolutely toward us.

"Hi, Pete," Lyle called out in recognition.

His official friend looked surprised to find *him* there. Since they hadn't seen each other recently, they did all of the talking: "Did you get an elk in Montana?" and so on.

Then duty called. "Mind if I check your licenses, fellas?" the conservation officer addressed Tommy and me. Lyle reached for his too, but his friend waved him off. Everybody checked out perfectly legal—except me. My error? I had the license, of course, and a federal duck stamp. But I did not have the *state* stamp.

"When I bought the license," I blurted, "they told me you don't need a state stamp to hunt on your own land."

"That's true," the unsmiling officer replied, "but you have to *live* on your land."

An awkward silence followed. All eyes were on me, the only criminal present. Suddenly I could hear the clank of a cell door. Fully aware that ignorance is no excuse in the eyes of the law, I mumbled something like "In that case, I'll be sure to get one."

To my relief, neither conservation officer pressed the point, and they turned to leave. I heaved a sigh and followed Lyle and Tommy toward the island, doubting if I would dare shoot at a duck now, even if they came over in droves.

I asked Lyle, "Do you think he would have fined me if you hadn't been there?"

He pondered a moment, and said, "Yes, I think he would've. He's a gung-ho game warden." And he elaborated: "One night I heard a shot in the woods about midnight. What else could that be? I called Pete, who lives about ten miles away on Tomahawk Lake, and he was at my place in fifteen minutes. I watched one road crossing and he came in from a different direction, but we couldn't find the poachers. I went home about 2:00 A.M., and Pete stayed out till morning, trying to catch 'em."

We need more dedicated game protectors like that.

I never shot another duck that fall. But I did learn, later on, that the young officer was in error; you do *not* need a state duck stamp to hunt on your own land, resident or otherwise.

* * *

At the ASCS office in Larsville, I ordered delivery of an aerial photo of our land. For $8.00 the government office in Utah would send me a 24″ by 24″ black-and-white print that covers one square mile.

Because my taxes had more than doubled in one year, I paid a call to the county courthouse. The assessor listened politely to my complaint before he filled me in on tricks of the trade in tax structuring.

"The state legislature forced us to reevaluate upward," he said, "due to escalating land values."

Inflation in this guise might appear beneficial, I acknowledged, but only to those who planned to *sell* their land.

To back up the official line of reasoning, the assessor showed me sale price figures of recent transactions. One party bought eighty acres and sold it within a year for twice the purchase price. But in that case, the county official and I agreed, the first seller was not aware of today's market values.

When the county assessor first discovered my shack in the woods, I braced for a tax increase. To be sure, my cherished shelter fell short of the "National Historic Monument" class. Still, I just knew that any building on undeveloped land had to invite a tax rise. But they reclassified it "seasonal recreation," and it gave me a jolt when the taxes went *down*. I didn't know whether to laugh or cry.

"The situation has just been changed," the assessor now continued. "Agricultural classification is now a lower tax rate than recreational. Therefore, because two-thirds of your front 40 is wetland (untillable), your tax will go down to one-third of last year's taxes on that portion next year."

That was encouraging, but in the next breath, he said, "Of course, taxes will go *up* next year on 'tillable' land."

I suggested that our state legislature is inclined to use the term "tillable" loosely in their comfy political fortress. How do you manage to till a woodland, unless you *first remove every tree?*

On the state level, officials certainly are not unaware of timber values. When the state sells land via county auctions, the land and timber values are listed separately. Sometimes the cost is divided

193

about equally, before sales tax is added to the transaction.

The assessor bounced me up again with "We'll look over your land to determine the total 'untillable' percentage for next year's evaluation." To me, it's *all* untillable, but that is not how the law works. At least an accurate estimate of the potholes and bogs might whittle down my tax in the future. That is, unless the state legislature does another flip-flop and *raises* the tax on "agriculture" class land . . .

After that stirring courthouse session, I needed the woodland solitude to help me sort out my options—if there were any left.

Back in camp, a wary grouse eyed me from the high limb of an aspen. At the moment, I might have traded worries with the woods bird.

21 In Quest of Venison

My heart's in the Highlands, my heart is not here,
My heart's in the Highlands, a-chasing the deer . . .
Robert Burns

The elusive whitetail intrigues me in any season. I never tire of watching a deer in its fluid bounding grace. And though it sounds paradoxical, I also find a superb challenge in the hunt. Matching wits with a wily old buck will test the mettle of any sportsman in a drama repeated over untold centuries.

The trees are dressed in reds and golds to celebrate a fruitful summer, and a kind of magic fills the air when October rolls around. The air turns cool and vibrant with expectation. Insects have felt the nip of frost, and the fragrance of autumn hangs over forest and field.

It is time to concentrate on the phantom whitetail. Deer season is only days away; you see it mirrored on the faces of your hunting friends. They begin to lose interest in major affairs of the world, and job performance slips a cog. Even the reality of family life blurs when a hunter's thoughts tend to focus on just one thing: "Will I bring home a deer this year?"

Traffic picks up on our lonely road in November. All types of truck, camper, car, and trailer rattle past on the night before the season opens.

This year, for the first time, I'll be hunting on my own land. Of course I have visions of venison steaks, even though I do not qualify as a "meat hunter" who glories in stuffing the deepfreeze.

Since I'm alone, I line up my gear in the shack and turn in early. During the night, brush wolves set off a wild cacophony of calls. Are they bemoaning the influx of human predators plotting to overrun their territory in the morning?

197

By 6:00 A.M., flashlight in hand, I set off in the predawn blackness. A spell of mild weather has left no tracking snow. With every cautious step I take, dry leaves crackle, telegraphing my approach to any deer within earshot.

I pick a stand by a clump of basswood and sit down. The silence is overwhelming, until I adjust to pure tranquility. In a world of darkness, I welcome the first hint of daylight, because dawn is the best time of day to observe the natural comings and goings of wildlife.

The November air is crisp and exhilarating, without any wind, and warm enough to rain. A ruffed grouse stirs in a nearby maple, and I come alive with its awakening. When daylight increases, the bird flies off in a rush to look for breakfast.

Woods watching hones my senses to a sharp edge. In the quiet of daybreak, I hear the rustling of a tiny shrew as it searches the leaves for worms and insects. The pointed snout of the little animal pokes out from under a leaf to check the air.

A shrew, though smaller than a mouse, has a voracious appetite. Due to its extremely high metabolism, it must eat almost continuously. It is claimed that a shrew's toxic bite can kill a cottontail rabbit.

But I am hunting bigger game. At last the sun's first rays light the treetops, and gray squirrels begin to chatter when the birds wake up.

In midmorning a misty haze develops and then turns into a gentle rain. I move deeper into the woods. If I don't get under a good-sized tree, my red coat will soon soak through. The spruce bog offers the best bet short of my hunting shack a mile away.

Before long I step into another world; plush moss underfoot cushions every step. I inhale the fragrance of wet evergreens, and a few yards into this primeval setting I pause to absorb the silent beauty. Not even the rain makes any sound here. I'm engulfed by greenery—balsam fir, spruce, and pines in all stages of growth. Only the tamaracks are bare until spring. A little red squirrel perches on a dead branch at eye level; he is quietly nibbling on a spruce cone. Nothing else stirs in this conifer cathedral.

Toward the middle of this haven, I find a thick spruce standing beside a tilted tree trunk. But before I reach its shelter, something catches my eye. A few steps away, almost hidden in a depression of wavy humps of moss, I discover a solid three-foot circle of pitcher plants. All are filled with rainwater.

Because of the drizzle, I can't stay long to marvel at this rarity. The spruce shelter beckons, and I slide under its layered branches for a superb setting to eat my lunch.

Light rain gradually turns to snow. I leave the spruce bog for open woods, and chance upon a drag trail. Backtracking, I find where someone has killed a buck. Proof positive hangs over a nearby limb. The pile of offal will make a feast for the ravens when they discover it, unless other scavengers get there first.

I move on to a knoll near a likely trail, and with my back against a tree, I become part of the forest. A black-capped chickadee lands on the end of my gun barrel. Dressed as always in his Sunday best, the little bird cocks his head to look into my face. He perches there only long enough to scold me in chickadee dialect, then flits away.

As I work my way farther back in the woods, I find drops of blood on the snow—a wounded deer. After two hours of slow tracking through the undergrowth, I come into our pine and spruce plantation. There the tracks and blood trail end—or at least I lose them.

Since the trail has led me toward camp, I cross the slough to the island. Not far off the old logging road, I spot a deer lying down, head alert. It is a doe. You're safe, I transmit silently to her—it's a "bucks only" zone. We stare at each other until she becomes unnerved. Abruptly she springs to her feet and bounds gracefully down the island out of sight. I wonder . . . Might as well take a look at the doe's bed. Sure enough, there is a trace of blood. Somebody made a "mistake." But the doe looks like a survivor, and she will probably give birth to a fawn in the spring.

In faint light of the second day, I pick my way along the hardwood ridge that overlooks the slough. A deer trail follows its lower edge. Once when I pause to listen, a grouse almost lands on my head. At the last instant the bird realizes its error and I feel a rush of air on my face from the furious beating of wings.

The warm, windless day makes the snow look out of place. After three hours of tense woods watching, I climb down from my tree stand to stretch. Nothing moving. I head back to the shack and build a platform step in front of the door. Then I make pancakes. Lethargy sets in, and a nap is in order. After all, what is a shack for?

In the afternoon, a few lingering mallards take off from the beaver backwater. Although thin ice covers most of the ponds, the ducks are putting off their trip south as long as possible. These stragglers have probably hatched here during the spring, and this will be their first migration.

In the hillside spruce planting, I come upon a roly-poly woodchuck. He isn't yet ready for his long winter snooze. Amongst the oaks, gray squirrels are busy hiding acorns, and here and there a ruffed grouse stirs my adrenalin. (Ask any deer hunter how many times the sudden noise of a rising grouse has brought on heart palpitations!)

The sun turns the snow to soft cake frosting, diffusing any evidence of deer movement. I relax in the warmth to eat a snack. A lone raven flies over, and his lazy wingbeats seem scarcely adequate to keep him aloft. The big black bird tilts his head and voices a hoarse croak at sight of me. Is he eyeing my sandwich?

I wander back to examine the firewood stacked in four-foot lengths. The cut ends are nicely checked after two years' drying time, and I wish for a magic wand to transfer a cord home for the fireplace.

Just as I climb onto a two-cord row of logs, I catch movement along the shoreline some thirty-five yards away—a mink on the prowl. I rest the butt of my rifle stock on top of the woodpile to watch his progress. Unhurried, he zig-zags in my direction. Along his route, each pile of wood has to be studiously examined—over the top, underneath, around the ends—no telling where a mouse or a rabbit might be hiding.

At last he reaches this stack of wood. A mink is a high-strung animal, and I wonder what his reaction will be when he catches sight of a human, or picks up my scent. I try not to move a muscle as the mink approaches my feet. There he stops to stare up into my face. I stare back at his smoldering ebony eyes. Since I make no sound or hostile movement, he continues on his search of this woodpile, too. His shiny dark fur is in prime condition.

While the mink is underneath the woodpile, I change position for a better view when he comes out. The sound of my boots up there does not escape his sensitive ears; I have to wait a few minutes before he dares show himself again.

Eventually the long, weasel-shaped body slinks out below my perch, as far away as possible. The mink scrutinizes me before proceeding to another pile of wood.

Finished with that, he chooses to cross the ice toward the beaver lodge out in front of me. I've often seen mink tracks in snow, but this time I have a ringside seat, a chance to watch the tracks being made. The warm day has made open patches of wet ice more slippery than usual, and the mink does some fancy skating before he gains solid footing.

The frozen beaver hut holds no interest for this predator. He dodges through ragged cattails and maneuvers around sticks packed into the beaver dam, and disappears on the slough island.

By nightfall I'm back in camp, tired and ready for a hot meal. The brush wolves howl again during the night, proclaiming their entitlement to the dark woods.

On the following weekend I bring along a partner, Ken's first trip to my woods. As we carry guns and gear into the shack, it begins to snow.

"Just what the doctor ordered," he grins. We hit the bunks about 1:00 A.M.

At 4:30 the alarm clock jangles us awake. *"Oh-h-h, boy!"* Ken groans at the short night. Just two words, but loaded with meaning. Never does he fail to start off a day of deer season that way. His drawn out "Oh-h-h, boy!" begins in midrange and slides into a low pitch. He drones it in a resonant bass that I understand to sum up: "Lordy it's cold climbing out of bed way before daylight . . . I could sleep three or four more hours . . . suppose we've got no choice, though, if we're gonna' try for a deer . . ."

After coffee we throw a pocket lunch together, load our guns, and start off by flashlight. Ken decides to stay close to camp until dawn, so he can figure out the lay of the land.

By the time I climb onto my favorite tree stand, faint daylight filters into the woods and an owl hoots at the passing of night.

An hour after sunup, I'm dressing out a hefty buck. Later, Ken saunters down the trail and smiles at the deer.

"How we gonna' get him out?" he puzzles.

"Lindstroms' cabin is less than half a mile from here," I tell him. "It's almost noon . . . somebody should be over there. I'll go see if those guys have a tractor."

When I top their hill and enter the grassy clearing, I hear them whooping it up in the cabin. Sounds like a rollicking poker game, but the boys are just having a beer break and lunch. Oscar swings open the door and waves: "Nothing hanging from the meatpole yet . . . you see any?"

"Yeah, a few does . . . and I got a nine pointer—"

The beer cans fly. Three wild-eyed hunters scramble for guns and jackets and light out for the woods. For a minute I'm afraid they'll *all* leave, and I'll be back where I started. But four of the seven remain for more details. In retrospect, I wonder if those three hunters that raced away knew what was coming.

"I didn't bring my little tractor up this week," Oscar laments.

The closest farmer lives about two miles away. What to do? Hunting fever grips them now, and nobody can offer assistance. For a few heavy seconds we all stare at the floor, until Oscar breaks the silence.

"Oh, why don't we give him a hand. We'll still have plenty of time to hunt. He says it's only about six hundred yards." (*Only?*) "We can carry it out in an hour." Bless his heart, I'm overwhelmed with gratitude.

It's a heavy animal, and we take turns carrying the deer Indian-style on a pole. For now the buck will be safe outside their cabin, well in from the road.

After supper in the shack, Ken and I haul the deer into town to be registered. Official field-dressed weight is 224 pounds. I enter the local contest, but at season's end a twelve-year-old boy wins the prize with a 248-pound buck—taken on his first deer hunt.

While we're registering, a man comes in scowling. "Damn deer jumped right out in front of me," he growls. "Spike buck."

The collision broke one of his truck headlights and damaged the fender and grill. It happened on the dark highway a few miles north of town, just minutes behind us.

*　　　*　　　*

On the last weekend of deer season, we're back for a final fling at filling Ken's license. I head out in the gray half-light of dawn, and a plump raccoon ambles across the trail ahead of me. He will soon be curled up inside a hollow tree, dozing away the worst of winter.

A windfall makes a good observation point on the hilltop. Presently a weasel comes by in search of a meal. He stops short at sight of me. His coat has turned to a fashionable white on schedule, and he poses pertly on his haunches, with front paws drooped below his chest. After a hasty appraisal of me and the surroundings, he hunches up and bounds off into the shadows.

The rut is on full tilt, and several buck scrapes turn up in the logging road. I spend the whole day in the woods, and in my wandering, select areas for firewood cutting. No other hunter crosses my path, but there is shooting off and on, not necessarily all at deer; maybe a potshot or two at a coyote, or a porcupine sunning on a limb, irresistible to some hunters. Once a boy whoops a victory yell—probably his first deer.

After sundown I come into the Lindstrom clearing. The hunters are all in for the night, and I stop to compare notes with them. This time I stay too long, because I left my flashlight beside a tree in the afternoon. Now I have to follow their winding driveway through pitch black woods for half a mile to the county road—and another half mile to the shack. It is the darkest of nights; I can't even see my feet. Every step has to be slow and deliberate to avoid twisting an ankle in the rutted road. The carrying strap on my rifle pays for itself this night.

The smell of woodsmoke cheers me as I reach our pulloff road. Muscle sore, worn to exhaustion, and *starved,* I at last trudge into camp. A golden square of warm light from the shack window beckons me "home."

My watch says 7:45, about three hours after sunset, and Ken hasn't even started supper. A boiled boot would have looked good to me right then, but Ken just isn't the kitchen type.

"Wasn't too hungry," he tells a starving man, "so I figgered to wait till you got back."

He hands me a snifter of brandy that gives me the needed voltage for frying a couple of fast hamburgers. Minutes later I plop onto the bunk.

Sleep does wonders. At 6:30 A.M. I crawl out to start breakfast and the noise jostles Ken awake. Another "Oh-h-h, boy!"

Today I'll cut across the lumpy new beaver dam where the busy engineers have shored up the natural pond. The air is sharp with frost, and it is impossible to walk quietly. My boots crunch frozen weeds, and ice crystals crackle and tinkle as I move across the island.

Near the stacks of firewood, five grouse burst out of the brush in a flurry, and farther down the trail, two big deer flag into thick cover. I study their tracks and conclude that they had been watching my noisy progress all along.

While I wonder why I didn't scope the edge of the woods from a distance, a sound gathers momentum from the opposite direction. A yearling bounds along the deer trail thirty feet away, between me and a thicket of alder. Following him, three more young deer charge past. All four are strung out a few yards apart, their tongues hanging out as if they've been running for some time. As the last one disappears into the spruce plantation, a lone buck makes one bound over a six-foot bush and vanishes. Seven deer in as many minutes, and I fail to fire a shot.

I retrieve my flashlight in the back woods, and in snow at the far side of the spruce bog, there are fresh tracks of two deer. A buck and his doe have slinked out ahead of me. I trace them over hills and through brushy gullies, but the romantic pair eludes me.

The woods are dark by the time I make the long trek back to camp. Another season has come to an end. Suddenly I'm weary from long days and short nights, and seized by a touch of melancholy. A whole year must pass before the stage will again be set for a chance at a whitetail. But next October, when the leaves begin to take on color . . .

*　　　*　　　*

Two weeks later, on our way to the shack, Ken and I took some

204

venison and deer sausage to Oscar's house. By now it was snappy cold outside, but the pressure was off, and we wouldn't have to get up before dawn tomorrow.

That evening, comfortably full of tender venison chops, we were toasting ourselves beside the barrel stove when the conversation turned to cougars. By some quirk of fate, both Ken and I had, on separate occasions, sighted mountain lions in the wilds of Minnesota. Spotting one of the big cats is a heart-stirring experience shared by very few people, and we are equally amazed at our good fortune.

During a deer season some years back, Ken saw his full-grown cougar cross a logging trail in Beltrami county. The rippling muscles and lithe grace of the huge cat left a lasting impression on him. As he describes it: "One of the most beautiful wild animals you'll ever see. It was such a pretty thing, I never even *thought* about raising my gun."

In my case, it was two young cougars still in the spotted stage. In 1952, while fishing on Caribou Lake near the Canadian border, I noticed the pair romping on the rocky shoreline. At first I thought they were foxes, but my binoculars proved otherwise. With an eight-millimeter camera, I took movies from the boat. To my undying regret, I had no telephoto lens—the young mountain lions were not discernible on film.

There were five in our fishing party, two women and three men, and we all watched the pair of cougars as long as possible. When they moved off the boulders and into the bushes, my fishing partner and I rowed over there, hoping to get a closer look at the wild kittens. That was foolish, expecting to see them again in heavy foliage. Nevertheless, we stepped quietly ashore.

Within seconds, on that windless summer day, we heard *one low growl.* How surprisingly fast we changed our minds about looking for cougars! The unseen mother lion may only have meant to alert her offspring to the threat of humans, but we jumped back into the boat and shoved off *muy pronto* to safety on the waters.

We reported our exciting morning to Carl Nelson, the resort owner, and he rasped: "Bobcats." In his fifty years of living up there in the wilderness, he had never been lucky enough to see a cougar.

When I returned to the city from that trip, I telephoned the head sportswriter of Minneapolis's leading newspaper. He listened politely but impatiently to my tale of sighting two young mountain lions. His flat comment? *"There are no cougars in Minnesota."*

In recent years, there have been other reports of mountain lions, most often in our northern counties, but proof is lacking; so far no one has come up with a photo of one. Ken and I cherish our once-in-a-lifetime sightings. It is extremely doubtful that either of us will ever again chance upon one of the rare and reclusive cats in the wild.

Just as Ken was launching into another story, there came a knock on the door. Seldom did we have night visitors at the shack. Ken cut off in midsentence, and our eyes met with a "surprised-by-the-game-warden" look.

Knowing we hadn't broken any laws, I stepped over and pushed the door open. The young man standing there came right to the point: "My battery went dead up the road aways; can you give me a boost?"

I invited him in from the cold, and discovered that he was not alone; two girls followed him into the shack, somewhat straining our living space. He gave his name, and I knew his father ran a business in Larsville. In fact, his dad owned land on the county road just north of us, and that was where the fellow's pickup had stalled.

Luck was with the three stranded travelers that frosty night. Purely by chance, Ken and I were "in residence" after deer season. Otherwise, the lightly dressed trio would have had to risk hypothermia by walking another mile or more for help.

We told the two shivering girls to wait there, and the three of us drove up to get the young man's truck started. Fifteen minutes later they were on their way.

After they'd gone, Ken and I had a good laugh as we described the look on the girls' faces when they first entered the shack. Neither one ever spoke a word in our presence, but they registered "what a messy place" when they stepped inside. We got the impression the girls were afraid the shack might fall in on them while we were gone. Or worse, they might pick up a terrible malady from these loony shanty dwellers. But "any port in a storm," and it kept them warm.

Since Ken and I were neighbors for years in the city, our wives are friends too. I told him I wouldn't tell *his* wife we had two fair young maidens in the shack if he promised not to tell *mine* . . .

Next morning we enjoyed the luxury of ignoring the alarm clock. After deer season, anything past 4:30 A.M. came as a bonus. I always get up before Ken, and I threw off the covers about 7:30. When I banged open the stove door to poke up the fire, Ken woke up.

"Oh-h-h, boy!" he groaned, and I knew some things never change.

22 Wild and Free

*I think I could turn and live with animals, they are so
placid and self-contain'd . . . they do not sweat and whine
about their condition . . . not one is dissatisfied.*
Walt Whitman

On a windy day in June, we turned onto the gravel road leading to
the wild 80. Near the place where Tommy and I once caught a
glimpse of a wolverine, a three-legged raccoon scooted across in
front of the car. One front foot was missing—a real hardship for the
animal's gathering of food, but regardless of his handicap, he looked
well fed. I stopped the car, and the 'coon watched us from the weedy
ditch, with only his bandit-masked face in sight.

Raccoons became scarce in the 1800s, when trappers and early
settlers made excessive use of the animal's flesh and fur. Davy
Crockett was not the only one to wear a coonskin cap. Protective
laws came much later, and now raccoons are plentiful again, even
around cities. In the country, where conditions are favorable, there
may be dozens of raccoons to a square mile. However, periodic
outbreaks of distemper can severely deplete the raccoon population.

For a while, a family of raccoons lived in the hollow of a huge elm
in front of our house. Every evening at dusk, the mother came out of
her den to make the rounds of neighborhood trash cans.

Once when I left a dead carp in the compost pit, I watched her
make the find. Though I never expected to see a fish in a tree, mama
raccoon dragged the carp up a big maple to feast.

After the baby 'coons had grown to traveling size, their mother
often led them through our yard after sundown. A raccoon's nimble
gait is unmistakable, traveling as it does with lowered head and
elevated haunches. On one occasion I saw her reclining in the crotch
of a backyard maple, nursing her young. She had five cubs, but up

209

there she could only service four at a time; the fifth one had to wait its turn.

A mature raccoon will dine on anything from insects to small mammals, but its summer diet is heavy on crayfish and frogs. The omnivorous animal can also be a scourge to nesting wood ducks. Raccoons are fond of certain fruits, such as pears. And anyone who has tried to raise sweet corn in 'coon country has cursed the masked marauders for the mess they make of the patch. Even so, the raccoon is seen as a fastidious animal, because it gives the impression of washing its food before eating. But I hold with the theory that raccoons were shortchanged on salivary glands, causing them to require extra liquid to aid digestion.

Sometimes late at night the neighborhood raccoon family disturbed my rest with their noisy screeching and chittering. One night when I heard the clanging of trash cans, I crept out and slammed on the lid. When I lifted the cover a crack, my flashlight revealed two young raccoons inside. They gave me a look of wide-eyed innocence. I placed a few bricks on top to hold them prisoner until morning; then I could get a good photograph of the mischief makers. They could eat in there all night if they chose.

Half an hour later, a *clang-bang* told me they had escaped. Those dexterous paws came in handy once again.

Later in the summer, a friend gave me a pair of banties. The little chickens aren't legal to keep where I live, but for awhile I would be able to hear the crow of a rooster at dawn—although it might befuddle our neighbors. Behind the garage, I threw together a wire mesh fence to form a chicken pen. The top was covered with fencing too, to discourage prowling cats and dogs.

The happy hen and the pompous rooster were an appealing diversion for about two weeks. Then one evening, just after dark, I heard a commotion out there. I shined a flashlight through the garage window, and wild eyes glowed. A big raccoon had its paws on the mesh, and two or three younger ones had the cage surrounded. The pair of banties were in a panic. I ran out to save them, but too late. As I rounded the corner of the garage, the beam of light caught the mother raccoon in the act of murder. The rooster had made the mistake of getting too close to the side, where the raccoon reached in

210

and grabbed him by the head. She was biting him in the neck for the coup de grace.

While the victim flopped on the ground inside the cage, I kicked and swatted coons in every direction, until they were all up trees. They still looked innocent as they chittered in complaint.

Realistically, I couldn't blame the family of raccoons; it was my fault for setting the table for them. I threw the dead rooster outside the pen, and reinforced the enclosure to protect the surviving hen.

Next morning, the hen was clucking for feed as if nothing had happened. Only a few feathers remained outside the pen to indicate that she ever had a partner.

*   *   *

We left the three-legged raccoon to his resources, and went on to the shack. The boys made a beeline for the ponds. Beavers had started another dam behind the island, and Alan compared his handprint with a cub-size bear track in the gooey mud.

A warm, steady breeze blew across the half mile of open slough, and throngs of last year's cattails bobbed and bowed toward us. On the edge of the woods, not thirty yards away, a pair of deer nibbled contentedly on tender tips of dogwood and hazel brush. Due to the wind rattling through the trees, the deer never became aware of us. We watched them until the forest of new green revealed only the flick of a white tail.

On the hillside conifer plantation, groundcover sprouts and grasses were emerging in the warm sun, and we happened upon a garter snake. Its forked red tongue darted out repeatedly to analyze the threat. The boys could not resist picking it up, in spite of the pungent odor these reptiles give off in defense-fright when handled. As soon as they released the harmless snake, it surprised us by regurgitating a small green frog.

"He's still alive!" we chorused.

The spotted frog looked bewildered with its harrowing experience. It took a few deep breaths before hopping away to enjoy a new lease on life.

I chose a shortcut back to camp through tangled alder and soggy

211

ground. A woodcock burst out at my feet and dodged erratically through brush and tree branches. It has been said that the "timber-doodle" must surely have been designed by a committee. His eyes are set too high on his head for him to enter any bird beauty contest, but that long proboscis serves him well for probing soft ground to reach earthworms. And those stubby wings offer more maneuverability than any engineer would think possible.

A snowshoe hopped away from the shack, and I noticed a hole under there. Did I have neighbors in the "basement"? As a rule, hares take shelter underground only in inclement weather, or when pursued by a predator; they do not care for living in burrows the way cottontail rabbits do.

Gail's friend had come along to camp with her in a tent. On a stroll down the gravel road, the little girls overtook a porcupine with a baby tagging behind. The young porky, about six inches long, bristled with miniature quills—a walking pin cushion. The girls knew better than to try petting it, but that didn't lessen their admiration.

"Dar-ling," they purred in unison.

*　　　　*　　　　*

In August I crawled out at sunrise and went down the road toward the hermit's 40. A young deer was browsing along the ditch across from the idle farm. I moved forward like a cat, only when the yearling's head was down, and crept within twenty-five yards of him.

After the deer reached the hayfield across from the hermit's place, his mood changed abruptly. From serious feeding, he switched to frivolity. Suddenly he began to prance across the field, periodically making short, joyful leaps into the air. Occasionally he would stop to survey the surrounding woods and, satisfied with himself, begin dancing again. If a deer is capable of pantomime, this one deserved applause for his "great-to-be-alive-on-a-summer-morning" portrayal. I enjoyed his antics until he melted into the far woods.

The pine seedlings in our clearing needed water. Thanks to Grampa's old scythe, I could mow down waist-high weeds for a trail to the nearest pond. When I set the heavy pails down to rest, I found a baby tree frog; he was hardly big enough to cover my thumbnail.

From the opposite side of the pond, a rust-brown doe was staring at me, with only her head and neck above the weeds. The deer studied me with intense curiosity before swapping ends to lope for cover. Her bushy tail flicked nervousness, but she could not resist taking one last look over her shoulder.

Pushing through tall weeds on a hot summer day stirred up mosquitoes thirsty for blood. I made a generous donation, but at least this species wouldn't repay me with malaria, as the *Anopheles* did in the South Pacific.

While I stood there, the soft hum of a dragonfly buzzed past my ear, and there was one less mosquito to bother me. Dragonflies were on my side; this oldest of flying insects can eat up to two hundred mosquitoes a day. The original dragonfly has not changed its biplane design in millions of years.

The wood ticks were not evident this late in the summer, and away from the ponds, there were fewer mosquitoes. I wiped my brow and went out to the road to catch the breeze.

As I leaned against the car, a reddish-colored fawn appeared in the ditch about fifty yards up the road. He came from the edge of the farm woods, and nibbled daintily on roadside bushes. His ears and tail flicked constantly to ward off flies; as he moved casually toward me, I waited to see how close he might come before picking up my scent. But the yearling changed course and crossed the road to my side. After he entered a small patch of trees and brush between our road and the ponds, the deer disappeared.

In such a limited area, (no more than twenty square yards) I thought for the fun of it I'd walk in and flush him out. But I could not find him anywhere. That little deer simply vanished! To this day I don't know how he managed to elude me.

Water, water, everywhere—and this time I forgot to bring any along. The farm pump across the road was out of service, so I drove down to Tomahawk Lake. At the wayside rest area pump, I filled two plastic jugs and a canteen with drinking water.

After my hard day's work, I stopped for a cold brew at the tavern overlooking the lake. It's a place where colorful characters quench their thirst, and I chatted with an older man called Buzz. One of his hands was covered with small wounds that were almost healed; I asked him what happened.

"Well-l, I'll tell ya . . . I was drivin' down a back road, an' I seen this animal run into the ditch. Never seen anything before quite like it. So I stopped the truck and got out fer a closer look. Thing had a long body, brown fur, an' short legs. I chased the cuss fer aways, and finally jumped on it to hold it down. Then I grabbed it with both hands . . . but the damn thing bit me a couple of times before I got a good holt of it. Put it in a box in my pickup, and brought it in here. Ever'body said it was a young otter."

The bartender verified his story. Other witnesses volunteered to back up Buzz. He said he never bothered to take rabies shots—not even tetanus.

Since otters are protected by law, I wondered what he did with the animal.

"Didn't hurt him as much as he did me," he laughed. "Kind of a purty little animal. I live near the river, so I took him down there and turned him loose. You shoulda' seen him take to the water, happy as can be."

I went back and tried to read the newspaper by lantern light, but the mosquitoes wouldn't leave me alone; I'd have to get under the bunk netting to be clear of them.

Did I hear a frog *inside* the shack? With the flashlight on him, he didn't make any sound, nor did he leap away. Fine. Let him start on the mosquitoes any time.

The visiting frog had a peculiar, offbeat breathing rhythm: one (pause), *two-three* (in rapid succession). I was afraid he might blunder into one of the mousetraps during the night, so I put him outside.

Next morning, I sat down on my homemade *kubbestuhl* to contemplate the new day. The chair's sudden collapse caught me off guard, and I fell off the stool. Part of the stump seat had rotted away, and crumbling wood exposed a nest of field mice; five pink, blind, hairless babies. Instinctively, they squirmed and wriggled to get away. One by one they fell to the ground. I gathered the tiny mice, nest and all, and put them into a tin bowl near the campfire for warmth.

214

Mother mouse had picked a suitably secret place to raise her young, away from the shack and the killer weasel. How could she anticipate such hazards as rotting wood and a lummox who would crush her hideaway? If the baby mice survived until dark, she would have a chance to move them to a safer place.

Another time, when we were a few miles from home, I glanced down at the windshield wiper blade on my side. Could I be seeing things? In the opening between the blade and hood, I thought I saw movement, and two beady eyes staring up at me. At first I dismissed it as impossible. And yet, I stole a look now and then at the open slot.

When I slowed down to wheel into the suburbs, a plump gray mouse stuck her head out to check the surroundings. Wind from the moving car rippled her fine coat of fur, and blew her guard whiskers to one side—literally a hair-raising ride. She popped out and ran across the hood at the base of the windshield and ducked into the slot on the right side. The boys let out a whoop: "Hey! Coo-ull-l!"

When we arrived home, I lifted the hood. No mouse in sight, but there was a nest built on a shelf behind the carburetor. Now she would have to start over in a new locale, and raise her young in the city.

*   *   *

Before setting off for the woods on a mild December morn, I fortified myself with a solid breakfast in the shack—eggs, pancakes, and honey.

Beyond the spruce grove, I came upon a skunk. Until he moved, his black-and-white pattern merged perfectly with snow and shadows. When we first met, the skunk showed more curiosity than consternation. I stood still, definitely not wanting to alarm him. Any confirmed woods wanderer soon grasps the advantage of remaining motionless while observing wildlife—especially this kind. Seeing no threat, the gentle-but-fearless animal continued foraging.

I have no quarrel with skunks in general; I find them interesting to watch in their natural surroundings. They are intelligent creatures, and are excellent mousers and insect-eaters. Energetic young skunks are especially charming. However, even the youngsters are packed

215

with pungency for their protection.

In my high-school days, a classmate became very attached to his pet skunk. The fellow pedaled his bike around town with the skunk riding in a wire basket ahead of the handlebars. His cycling passage caused some alarm for pedestrian strangers who did not know the skunk had been descented.

And some years ago, my friend Don found a skunk blundering blindly across a field with its head stuck in a tin can. The animal's helplessness aroused Don's sympathy; but should he risk removing the can? Win or lose, he opted to take a chance. First he took a long stick and tried to pry off the can. That didn't work; no leverage. There was only one thing to do—bend down and get hold of the can itself.

As gently as possible, he carefully tugged and twisted the can until it came loose. The skunk was free! Don stepped back, prepared for the worst—a release of pent-up animal frustration. But the liberated skunk just blinked in the sunlight and appraised his benefactor. Don backed slowly away, with a sigh of relief when the skunk ambled away in peace.

The most serious complaint against skunks, of course, is their notorious facility for harboring rabies. I wondered now about the trim and tidy animal before me. Could he be afflicted? If he had acted in any way abnormal up to this time, I certainly would not have pursued the issue.

I could not be sure of this full-grown skunk's mood. Camera ready, I edged closer. Heavy boots in crunchy snow took away any chance of stealth. When he stopped, I stopped. The skunk's bushy plume of a tail stayed high. Caution. I only wanted a picture, not a malodorous memento. Other animals (usually predators) and humans have been temporarily blinded by the full force of skunk spray.

After a few of these stop-and-go sessions, the animal turned to face me. He leaned back slightly and struck the ground with both front paws. I froze while he paused to wait for my reaction. We stared at each other. Since his petulant demonstration didn't frighten me off, he elevated his rear end a trifle. He was still facing me, but skunks can fire an overhead salvo from this position with deadly accuracy. I stood motionless and relied on my nonaggressive posture.

216

His pointed nose twitched to decipher my scent, though I could not detect his odor. Presently he moved on at a leisurely pace, and I followed.

By this time the skunk showed signs of annoyance at being trailed on his rounds. He turned abruptly and made a short dash toward me—and stopped. I stood my ground where I hoped to be out of his twelve-foot range. Even then, if he should let fly with his not-so-secret weapon, the fetid fumes could permeate the air all around me. I can think of no other smell that lingers so long or travels so well on the wind.

For the life of me, I don't know how my dad and uncle were able to stand it during the Great Depression. They dug out skunk dens and skinned the putrid carcasses to collect a dollar per hide. Of course in those days a dollar was a dollar, and men put in ten hours of labor for just one buck. Today's teenagers would laugh their heads off at such rates.

While facing me, the potential stinker grunted two or three times and hit the ground again with his front paws. When that brought no reaction from his two-legged nemesis, he raised his hind quarters off the ground in a hopping motion. Oh-oh . . . had I pressed my luck too far?

I gambled on it being just another bluff, because skunks use their defensive fluid sparingly. Nevertheless, I stayed behind a tree, and reached around the trunk to take his picture. The click of the shutter sent him off at a faster clip.

Hoping for one more picture, I trotted parallel to his movement along the shoreline of the slough; only then did I catch the faint whiff of skunk. Suddenly he stopped short. So did I, believe me. Enough of this nonsense—the skunk charged straight at me! For a second I thought of dropping the camera and drawing my target pistol. No need for that, I quickly decided; I'd outrun him if necessary.

Once more, the skunk halted twenty feet away and went through his warning routine. Then, finding no real danger to his welfare, he wheeled and put on speed toward the frozen slough. I ran up and snapped a broadside shot of him hightailing it over the snow-covered ice.

Epilogue

I've always been captivated by the activity of any wild animal or bird in its natural surroundings. Most people are, I suppose, satisfied with a visit to the zoo. That is accepted as the civilized way to get close to animals, mainly exotic species from other countries. But studying a caged beast is not the same as watching an animal free in the wild. Behind bars for a life sentence, zoo animals lose their flair for survival.

Even the latest trend in zoos, extended land in simulated native conditions, can never equal the real thing. And yet, some animals' earthly existence can only be preserved by holding them captive. Objectively, maybe "half a loaf is better than none."

Not everyone can understand the cultural value of wilderness. Some people perceive such places as uncivilized wastelands. Wilderness—and thereby habitat for wildlife—has been under assault since the first pilgrims arrived. As the twentieth century winds down, untamed land and its attendant wildlife get short shrift in the drive to increase the gross national product. Unfortunately, shortsighted greed still threatens our shrinking wild preserves.

Most of America's wetlands have been drained in the name of progress. Ignored in the process are the watershed benefits of flood control, rejuvenation of groundwaters, and wildlife habitat. Meanwhile, an appalling tonnage of topsoil goes down our rivers every year. Also, many thousands of acres of productive and marginal land

219

have been gobbled up by highways and urban development, with no end in sight.

The seesaw of political influence and a mushrooming population continue to chip away at the world's remaining unspoiled land. In the recent race for the U.S. presidency, the subject of ecology barely surfaced. Political leaders of the 1980s have shoved environmental concerns onto the back burner—but even there the unwatched pot will boil over. Conservation-minded presidents like Theodore Roosevelt do not come around often. In this age, can you imagine *him* opening millions of acres of public park land in the West to commercial exploitation?

It is high time to ask ourselves, "What are we doing to our planet?"

The slaughter of whales continues, now under the guise of "scientific research." Adding insult to injury, the oceans are being polluted with toxic wastes. Disposal of dangerous chemical by-products is an unsolved dilemma. Doubtful pesticides and other untested chemicals are turned loose year after year. We'll find out the hard way if they have unsafe side effects, or prove not biodegradable.

Too much faith is placed in technology. Instead of solving all of our problems, technology may yet turn us into its victims.

Misguided industrial and agricultural practices are altering the health of our planet—permanently. Not many years ago, most of us had never heard of the ozone layer in outer space. Scientists now warn of the potentially life-threatening "greenhouse effect," warming the earth and changing climates. Pollutants accumulating in the stratosphere have begun to eat away the earth's shield against ultraviolet radiation. The chickens may be coming home to roost.

To date, scant political attention is being paid to curbing the threat of acid rain, other than suggesting "more studies." In the U.S.A., some lakes have already been pronounced devoid of life. And German citizens are bemoaning the death of trees in their Black Forest; they blame acid rain brought on by industrial pollutants. Other countires will be heard from, to be sure.

The mindless rape of the rain forests is one of the most disturbing abuses of natural resources. In Brazil, for instance, impoverished people are cutting and burning hundreds of acres every day. The thin tropical soil will not support crops for very long, and the people then push on to yet more destruction. The rain forest cannot replenish itself—when it is gone, it's gone.

Much of the world's oxygen is supplied by those trees, and does some yet undiscovered jungle plant offer a cure for cancer or other maladies? If rain forests are reduced to photographic memories, we'll all be the poorer for it.

All of which points to the major problem of overpopulation, especially in the undeveloped "third world" countries. The earth now holds *five billion people,* and the population is expected to double early in the next century. As the quote goes: "We have met the enemy and he is us."

Answers to these ecological dilemmas are begging for attention. What can we do? For starters, let us press for better education worldwide. We must also keep a sharp voter's eye on our representatives at both state and federal levels. Join or contribute to any of several national organizations dedicated to protecting the environment. Our children and grandchildren deserve to inherit a healthy environment, not a legacy of waste and pollution.

There is much to gain by studying one remote patch of woodland, as I've tried to point out in these chapters. Still, you need not *own* a chunk of land to find solitude, or to observe nature. There is some kind of rejuvenating retreat within reach of us all in this vast country.

There have been changes in the wild 80 . . . Our siblings have turned into teenagers and beyond, with varying lifestyles, but I'm sure they cherish woodsy memories.

The shack stands empty now, except for the roosting birds that find ready access. And a cottontail lives beneath the rotting floorboards, where he shares residence with a woodchuck. (The "groundhog" sleeps all winter, anyway.) We've since built a genuine cabin, complete with porch.

New neighbors border our backwoods, and more hunters tend to get "lost" during the season—some accidentally, some on purpose.

A logging crew is cutting aspen and thinning the hardwoods. Deer and snowshoe hares were quick to find the bountiful source of winter food. For a while, coyotes were decimating rabbits, but now both hares and grouse are on an up cycle. Just recently, coyote numbers took a plunge—quite possibly due to an epidemic of mange mites. Mother Nature has her way of balancing the books.